PHOBIAS
AND
OBSESSIONS

PHOBIAS
and Obsessions

Their Understanding and Treatment

JOY MELVILLE

London
UNWIN PAPERBACKS
Boston   Sydney

First published in Great Britain by
George Allen & Unwin 1977
First published in Unwin Paperbacks 1979

UNWIN® PAPERBACKS
40 Museum Street, London WC1A 1LU

© Joy Melville, 1977, 1979

British Library Cataloguing in Publication Data

Melville, Joy
  Phobias and obsessions.
  1. Phobias
  I. Title
  616.8′522   RC 535

ISBN 0-04-150070-9

Printed in Great Britain by
Hunt Barnard Printing Ltd.,
Aylesbury, Bucks

CONTENTS

INTRODUCTION

'From where I sit,' wrote Sylvia Plath, 'I figure the world is run by one thing and this one thing only. Panic with a dog-face, devil-face, hag-face, whore-face, panic in capital letters with no face at all – it's the same Johnny Panic, awake or asleep.'

Johnny Panic is present in the lives of an estimated four million phobics in Britain alone. Acute panic causes sweating, palpitations, faintness and paralysis of movement. Phobics suffer from such sensations whenever they are in the situation they fear; and these sensations can be so strong that they often believe that they are having a heart attack, going mad, or are just not normal.

One of the main needs for a book like this is to make phobics realise that their fears are *shared*: that they are not alone either in what they fear or in how they react to it. Phobics feel their phobia is something unacceptable; something impossible to explain; something to be ashamed of. While researching the book I was constantly told, 'Please never mention my name'; 'I wouldn't want anyone round here to know'; and, above all, 'People think you are mental'. Most were quick to cite their education, or their job, as proof that, phobia notwithstanding, they were intelligent and capable. Many were too ashamed of their fear even to reveal it to their doctor, convinced that he would not understand and would merely laugh.

There is, indeed, a general lack of understanding about phobias, not just by many doctors, but also by the relatives and friends of phobics. What is also needed, and what I have tried to do, is to make non-phobics appreciate the depth of fear involved by showing, in the phobics' own words, the effect it has on their lives. Only by this understanding and co-operation can the phobic be helped. But, in general, friends react to phobias with amusement or frank disbelief; and relations, who naturally see more of the effect it has, are puzzled and irritated. A marriage, in particular, can be put under great strain – especially in the case of agoraphobia, when one partner's fear of going out can jeopardise the whole relationship.

But as well as understanding, phobics also need practical help.

And the great majority do not know where to turn for advice or treatment. They do not know what treatment exists, where to get it or what it is like. ('Is it true they throw you in a room with hundreds of spiders?' one spider phobic asked me.) Sometimes they tolerate their fear until it precipitates a crisis or causes their lives to become impossibly restricted. Or they will shop around for treatment on a hit-or-miss basis.

This book is intended to help anyone suffering from a phobia by showing them, in layman's language, the kinds of treatment that are available for different phobias. (The word 'phobia' comes from the Greek *phobos*, which means extreme fear, terror. It is an excessive, irrational and uncontrollable fear of perfectly natural situations or objects.) I have given as broad a picture as possible by having psychologists and psychiatrists talk about their methods, combined with phobics' own reactions to different kinds of treatment and the results of research into treatment. The appendix at the back lists the addresses of various organisations and societies which will be of help.

Above all, I have tried to give phobics an optimistic, positive approach by showing how other phobics have managed to overcome their fears to a greater or lesser extent, and by describing the methods of self-help many have used. Phobics need reassurance, particularly in the case of the most common phobia, agoraphobia, which many of its sufferers simply do not understand. When its onset is explained, their fears are often immediately lessened. Housebound agoraphobics, who feel particularly despairing because they cannot leave the house to get treatment, can see how to practise certain self-help methods at home, on the lines of the type of treatment they would get at a clinic.

To contact phobics, I had a letter published in *Woman* magazine, which brought some 300 replies; and a note in *She* magazine, which had about two dozen replies. I also advertised in some local London papers (about 30 replies); in New York's *Village Voice* (a dozen or so replies); a French newspaper (some 20 replies); *New Society* (8 replies); the Open Door newsletter, a correspondence club for agoraphobics (about 30 replies); plus some 40 letters arising from a

Reading *Evening Post* column which mentioned the book. The *Sunday People* published an article called 'My secret fears', inviting readers to write in with them, and kindly let me see the 200 or so replies it received. I also had information and help from Katharine Fisher, founder of The Phobics Society; Alice Neville (now retired) of The Open Door; Mona Woodford, who now runs the re-named Open Door Association; and Vanna Gothard, of the smaller Phobic Trust.

In addition, I went to New York to see the methods being used there to treat phobics. Although the average American still goes in for psychoanalysis more than his British counterpart, several clinics have now opened in New York which concentrate on behaviour therapy techniques. A little more emphasis was placed on group rather than individual therapy; and those I spoke to at two groups of 'mixed' phobics had found that listening to other phobics' problems and their methods of tackling these was particularly helpful. The large number of women's groups in New York – from 'consciousness raising' ones to women's lib – give the women, at least, a chance to talk over their problems (phobic and others) and get support from each other. Some cannot communicate with their partner; as Dr Alexandra Symonds shows in her pamphlet *Phobias after Marriage*, a phobia like agoraphobia is often deeply bound up with the marital relationship.

I have also included a chapter on compulsive obsessions, as obsessions and phobias are both defences against anxiety. There is often a strong phobic element present in obsessions – a fear of germs, for instance, being a factor in compulsive handwashing – and the behaviour therapy treatment is on similar lines to that used with phobics. Again, this condition can place a tremendous strain on relationships. The obsessive, like the phobic, is at pains to conceal his obsession, believing the reaction will be one of amazement.

Both male and female phobics and obsessives can realise from this book that treatment can be successful, and that too many share their feelings for them to consider themselves an embarrassing oddity.

I

Agoraphobia or the Fear of Open Spaces

'I remember walking up our street, the moon was shining and suddenly everything around me seemed unfamiliar, as it would in a dream. I felt panic rising inside me, but managed to push it away and carry on. I walked a quarter of a mile or so, with the panic getting worse every minute. By now I felt totally unreal, as if I was watching some terrifying film of myself walking along the streets. There was no sign of my husband, whom I was meeting, and I stopped on the corner of the main road. I stood up against the fence as I felt very faint. Two people came along and I almost stopped them to ask if they could see me – was I really there?

'I decided I must try to keep moving and walked with difficulty to the next road junction. By now I was sweating, yet trembling; my heart was pounding and my legs felt like jelly. I felt I could go no further – as if another step would take me over the edge into some dark pit. Terrified, I stood, not knowing what to do. The only bit of sanity left in me told me to get home. Somehow this I did, very slowly, holding on to the fence along the road. I cannot remember the actual journey back, until I was going into the house, then I broke down and cried helplessly . . . I did not go out again for a few days. When I did, it was with my mother and my baby to my grandmother's a few miles away. I felt panicky there and couldn't cope with the baby. My cousin suggested we go to my aunt's house, but I had another attack there, this time with shooting pains all through my body. I was sure I was going to die. I was certainly very close to fainting and the panic was uncontrollable. Following this, I was totally unable to go out alone and even with someone else I had great difficulty. Not only did I get the panicky-fainting spells, but I lived in constant fear of getting them.'

Agoraphobia usually starts this way: in the form of a quite unexpected attack of panic. The sensations experienced can be overwhelming: pounding heart, dizziness or fainting, palpitations, sweating, or a sense that 'something' terrible is about to happen. Most people interpret these sensations as 'symptoms' and are convinced they are going mad, or having a heart attack. This is understandable, from some of the descriptions I heard: 'It was at first like living in a nightmare; all the time, the fear of almost everything. One afternoon, I convinced myself I was going to die. I started to go hot and cold, then shake from head to foot. My heart started to beat faster and faster and I was sure I was going to faint, but I did not: now if I go out I must always be with someone.' 'It's an all-consuming sensation which paralyses my mind and body and makes me want to rush to the nearest house and take cover.' 'I got chest pains and my feet felt as if they were nailed to the floor.'

After such experiences, fear naturally sets in, but it is a fear of these *sensations* happening again. And, possibly helped by nervous expectation, they do occur again. The first attack may have taken place anywhere (in the street, supermarket, lift, even the home itself); succeeding attacks are equally unpredictable. The result is that the person concerned only feels safe inside, or near, the house. The thought of another public panic attack – particularly if it involves fainting and an ambulance being called – is acutely upsetting. The agoraphobic can have an increasingly restricted life and may even end up by being totally housebound. As one said: 'I have put my coat on hundreds of times and got as far as opening the door and standing on the doorstep. But I can't go any further. You get this fear in your body and it puts you in a panic. If somebody speaks to you, you can't answer them because nothing will come and so the panic gets worse. The further you go away from the house, the worse it gets.'

Agoraphobics react differently to a panic attack, but most feel frightened, unable to move, or so weak-kneed that they have to hold on to someone or something for support, or fall. What is important – and which is stressed by Dr Victor Meyer at Middlesex Hospital – is that agoraphobics should not try to fight a panic. If they give in to it, it will pass more easily. Trying to fight it only emphasises it. It is also important for an agoraphobic to accept that he may have to live with these panic attacks for some time – until his latent stress is cleared up. Sometimes an agoraphobic may go for months without an attack, and think he is cured – then unexpectedly have another one and succumb to depression and retreat inside the house.

Agoraphobics need to accept these panic attacks in the way they would have to accept diabetes – that is, a condition which they just have to live with and adapt to. By accepting the fact that, on the way to the shops, they may quite well have a panic attack, perhaps two, and that it will be embarrassing and very upsetting, *but that is all*, they will put their fears into proportion. They may feel as if they are going to die, but they will not. For example, the elderly mother of one agoraphobic lost her temper with her daughter who, on a walk, kept saying she felt terrible and was going to die, and snapped: 'Well, *die* then.' The daughter then found she could not even manage to feel faint.

Usually agoraphobics associate their fear with the place where it first happened – agoraphobia means 'fear of the market place', from the Greek word *agora*. They feel that by avoiding this place, they will stop the fear. But it is sheer chance where these panic attacks take place, because they are caused by an accumulation of over-anxiety and stress. This, in turn, causes the nervous system to fire off fiercely, making the body go into a state of heightened activity – heart-pounding and so on. Few people realise that these sensations, however frightening, are in fact harmless – indeed they are signs that their nervous system is in good working order, and is merely summoning up resources to fight the 'crisis' signs of stress. This stress may have been building up for months or years due to pressures like poor housing, crowded supermarkets, money troubles and family relationships. Or it may have been caused by a recent calamity.

Agoraphobia is sometimes called 'the calamity syndrome' as so often it appears after a severe shock, an operation or a change of lifestyle – like getting married, or having a baby. I found in talking to agoraphobics that shock was high on the list of causes. Some of these were traumatic. One women, for instance, saw a window cleaner fall from the top storey of a high building, almost right in front of her. When she next went into that street, she had a panic attack which gradually spread to *all* streets. A similar incident happened with another phobic, when a drunk fell down and severely cut himself on the pavement, and left her with a fear of going out on her own. An Englishwoman, now living in the United States, said her agoraphobia had started after being caught in an earthquake. And a twenty-year-old girl had the shock of being jilted at the altar. After this she stayed indoors, convinced that the neighbours were whispering about her; and finally would not leave the house at all.

The death of a parent, or of a marriage partner, also figured largely as a precipitating factor, often compounded by other upsets. Queen Victoria may well have been an example of this. Several elderly people mentioned to me that they could not cope with the strain of busy streets and shops without their partner. With one woman in her twenties, agoraphobic symptoms began when her divorce was followed by the death of her mother, to whom she was very close. A double shock of this kind had a similar effect in another case, where the shock of a father's death was combined with a bad bout of influenza. In later years, the person concerned had to go into hospital with back trouble and this caused her phobic symptoms to grow considerably worse. Even phobics who have been managing to get around reasonably well after treatment can quickly revert to staying inside after a spell of being indoors. They can also revert when faced with any further shock or emotional upset.

Agoraphobics are unable to explain why this phobia should set in after they have got (happily) married or had their first or second (longed-for) child. But obviously in some cases, this must have caused more stress than they realised. One doctor in Harlow New Town told me that his surgery is full of women who were suffering from hypertension and were potential agoraphobics. This was mainly a result of leaving parents, friends and familiar surroundings and having to make new friends, assess new schools, and have no one to mind the children.

Another contributory factor was mentioned by Dr Alexandra Symonds, author of the pamphlet, *Phobias after Marriage*, who said that many of the women patients she sees, including well-adjusted professional women, had one thing in common: they did not confront either themselves or their husbands with their ordinary irritation. The phobia, she considers, is most of the time a repressed anger.

One theory about agoraphobia is that it can be a subconscious safeguard *against* a fear, or failure – a way of avoiding carrying out certain duties or tasks, and a protection against these. (Though agoraphobia is a heavy price to pay.) One man, for instance, used it as a protection against getting married: 'We'll marry when you're better,' his fiancée kept saying. Another man – a caretaker, with a history of nervous trouble – said that the onset of his phobia was during the last war, on service in the Middle East. Some German planes had come over, strafing, and afterwards he found he could not look up into the sky. Further sensations developed: a sense of choking and the feeling his legs were going to give way under him. He was then sent home. Now he wonders whether his phobia was the result of a subconscious desire to get out of the battle zone. In another case, a married woman who found herself unable to go shopping admitted to feeling attracted by the butcher's assistant. Her shyness and anxiety about this resulted in her developing a phobia as a protection. Knowing the probable reason, however, did not help her to overcome the phobia.

Agoraphobia can also be used, subconsciously, as a reason for *not* taking that better job, or, indeed, *any* job; or not having to leave the security of the home and go out, especially in a strange district; or not having to socialise. If you ask an agoraphobic for a list of things that he or she would like to do most if they were free of the phobia, this could reveal precisely what the phobic does not really want to do and was using the phobia to avoid. However, they might be quite unaware of this themselves.

An American college boy illustrated this. He was criticised in class, lost control and started screaming at the teacher. After that, he developed fears which were a mixture of claustrophobia and agoraphobia. He stopped taking certain classes and became increasingly worried about going to college, or to downtown Manhattan. His agoraphobia was a protection from these fears.

His psychologist, Dr Leonard Bachelis, Director of the Behavior Therapy Center in New York, agreed that the boy's anxiety basically stemmed from being away from the safety of home, and was compounded by the fact that he felt that he could save his parents from splitting up if he stayed at home and kept the family united. To help his anxiety in the classroom and his relationships with classmates and teachers, Dr Bachelis employed assertive training therapy. 'I tried to stop him from being intimidated,' he said. 'If he was asking a girl for a date, for instance, he shouldn't say, "Do you think you might want to go out with me, maybe, please?" He should simply ask if she would like to go out on a specific night, at a specific time. He also felt very scared and unreal looking at large buildings, and wanted to get away. In such situations, he was not sure whether he was awake or asleep. We managed that by him imagining that he was outside in the street in pyjamas and we did some role-playing. I acted the part of a passer-by, saying: "What's wrong with this crazy guy?" He struck back by replying: "What's wrong with you, haven't you ever seen anyone in pyjamas before?" That way we brought out the worst situation he could envisage, of thinking himself sleeping and actually being awake in the street.' 'I felt much more confident after imagining this,' said the boy. 'I think imagining things helps most, and just being able to share problems. Before I might just mention to my best friend that I didn't like Manhattan; but I wouldn't tell him why, for fear I'd be laughed at. After imagining the worst situation a number of times, I felt able to handle my fears and they then went away.'

The strain that being virtually housebound imposes on both the phobic and his or her family is, naturally, immense. As Isaac Marks says, in *Fears and Phobias*: 'The fluctuating nature of agoraphobia makes it difficult for family and friends to accept that it is an illness and not the result of laziness, lack of will-power, or a way of getting out of awkward situations.' This feeling of not being understood was stressed by many agoraphobics. One said: 'People don't realise how much agony of mind people like us go through: pain in the body is nothing compared to it.

'They just tell you to pull yourself together, help yourself. Why don't they realise it's like telling a man with a broken leg to get up and walk?' Her feelings were echoed by other phobics: 'The men in my life, having never understood for a moment how one feels at times, either scoff or jokingly say that one is going round the bend, which is the last thing a sufferer wants to be told'; 'People think it is just sympathy and attention you are after: I have been dished out a lot of criticism, but I must add that I was of the same opinion before I became agoraphobic myself'; 'How can people understand? You look fine, sometimes you look a lot better than the people around you – even though you might have legs as heavy as lead, and the ground might be moving.'

The marriage partner is, naturally, particularly affected. The husband of one agoraphobic told me that he had often gone straight from work into a pub. 'I knew once I got home there'd be no going out again, no escape.' (His wife retaliated by saying, 'He's got one advantage. I can't haunt him when I die, as I won't dare leave the coffin.') Many marriage partners are extremely sympathetic and understanding. But agoraphobia is very complex – and can be the result of a balance-of-power struggle between the partners, even if this is quite subconscious. If a husband 'cannot' go out in the evenings, because he feels obliged to stay in and keep his wife company, his wife may feel more secure. That way he cannot meet other women socially, or spend most of his time at the pub. The children, too, may stay around more to help – sometimes even to the extent of not leaving home so quickly for a flat of their own. Not that such consideration can be taken for granted. 'My husband never takes me out,' said one wife. 'He likes a drink, and I don't like to keep my children in for company, so I get left quite alone most nights.'

The phobic is, however, the focal point of the family. One psychologist said that, in his experience, 'You nearly always find an established situation – women sitting in their houses, usually with anxious husbands, children or parents saying, "There, there, don't you worry; are you near enough to the television?" One feels their life would be much more uncomfortable without it.' And another told me that a woman agoraphobic admitted to him that if she got better, she knew her husband would leave her – a fact confirmed to him by the husband. If the agoraphobic is getting a certain reward from his or her curtailed life, treatment will naturally not succeed, or else be very gradual. Eric Berne, in *Games People Play*, considers people play out their neuroses in 'games' – and the essential feature of a game is its pay-off. In agoraphobia, a relevant game is If-It-Weren't-For-You. In this, a woman marries a domineering man so that he will restrict her activities and so keep her out of situations which frighten her. But instead of thanking him, she complains about the restrictions, which makes her spouse feel uneasy and gives her all sorts of advantages.

A husband may not necessarily object to being called upon to cope with all the extra problems his wife's agoraphobia causes – such as, say, taking the children to school. He is aware of his wife's ever-increasing dependency on him, and this boosts his masculinity. 'You can often tell the situation as soon as you go into a phobic's home,' said one therapist. 'The other day I went back with one woman agoraphobic, and her husband jumped up as we came in, and said, "I don't suppose she's much better, is she? Now you both sit down and I'll get the tea." You could tell that he wasn't really pushing his wife to get better; that he was rather enjoying himself.'

Some husbands may need this dependence, emotionally. In one exceptional case, a woman with reasonably severe agoraphobic symptoms found it almost impossible to travel by bus, and her husband drove her everywhere. With treatment, she gradually improved; and two months later her husband killed himself. It had turned out that, once she no longer needed him, he felt overshadowed. Sometimes patients know that the marital relationship cannot take such a change. Either they will go through treatment and not improve, or they will improve and the relationship will become disturbed – as they had known it would. When a group of women agoraphobics recently improved substantially after treatment at a psychiatric hospital, three of the husbands became impotent. One wife, realising this was tied up with her newfound ability to go outside the home – presumably now a threat to the husband, who felt he could lose her – quickly developed 'back trouble' instead. The marriage reverted, successfully, to its old dependence relationship. Sometimes this dependence relationship can get too overpowering, when the phobia spreads from being unable to go out, into being unable to be alone with such anxiety. In one case, the husband had to change from working in an office to working at home, because his wife would run after him in her nightdress in the mornings, terrified at being left alone.

But although an element of manipulation can come into agoraphobia, most of the phobics would refute any suggestion that they are contributing to the situation – being all too aware of the damage it is doing to their lives. 'It causes terrible problems,' said one housewife, who has had agoraphobia for eight years. 'The children miss out on lots of things, as I can't take them around to parties and so on; and my husband has to take time off to take them to dentists, doctors and so on. He does all the shopping, and this makes life hard for him. I am in the house all day on my own, with only the dog to talk to, and feel that I am really going mad. The house is like a prison: all I do all day is housework, to keep myself busy. Having agoraphobia makes one very, very lonely as you can't go out to see anyone. If only I had someone to talk to, it wouldn't be so bad.'

'The effect it has on my life has been disastrous,' said another woman. 'I mind very much putting the burden of shopping on my young daughter; the loneliness, the torment that goes on inside. You can't imagine what it's like.' And a housewife with an eighteen-year-old daughter, said: 'If my daughter asks me to go anywhere with her, I just make excuses. I long to meet her from work and go shopping or have a coffee or lunch with her, but I just can't do it. I feel I must let my husband have some outlet, so he goes out for a drink. But that's all the pleasure he has. He would have loved a bigger family, but I stopped that; he would like to move, but I just can't go where I don't know anyone. At present we are on our holidays . . . but I can't go anywhere.'

A nationwide survey of over 1,000 agoraphobics was carried out in 1975 at Sparthfield Clinic at Rochdale, Lancashire, by L. E. Burns and G. L. Thorpe. Some 90 per cent of the agoraphobics were housewives, although half of them felt they would like to take a job outside their home were it not for their condition. Only very few were divorced, but half of them felt that agoraphobia was putting a strain on their marriage. Again, half felt the condition came on insidiously, though in most cases it was precipitated by a particular incident, such as feeling faint in town, or an accident.

In a previous survey held in 1970 by I. M. Marks and E. R. Herst (*A Survey of 1,200 Agoraphobics in Britain*), it was found that most rated their condition as 'a nuisance, but I can cope'. Again, 95 per cent were women and the average length the phobia lasted was 13 years. Once the phobia began, 80 per cent were never completely free of it again.

In this survey, everything pointed to discontented housewives being more severely ill than contented ones. Their phobias and associated symptoms were more severe; they were more depressed and exhausted; they were worse when they were alone; and their need for help was greater – yet they more often could not get it.

Most of the 1,200 agoraphobics had gone to their doctor for help; and two-thirds had had some form of psychiatric advice (usually about 18 months after first going to the doctor). Only when this failed to help did a small minority finally go to a spiritual or faith healer. A tiny proportion had never had treatment at all and these were distinctive for their lack of social confidence, an inability to confide in anybody, and a slowness to ask for help, not just from doctors, but from any source. In general, they kept their feelings to themselves.

In this way, they resembled many male agoraphobics. A woman

can suffer from 'nerves' and stay at home, but it is not socially acceptable for the man to do so – and probably not financially possible, either. The men will therefore use a number of strategies to prevent their phobia from crippling their life. One company director, for example, successfully conceals his agoraphobia by being met at the door each morning by his chauffeured car, and getting straight out into the doorway of his office building the other end; and similarly, for lunch. (Agoraphobics feel 'safe' in a car, which is like another small house, although they often do not like going too far from their home.) Another man cannot go further from his country house than a radius of 100 yards. Not wanting to ask anyone else to take his dog for a longer walk than this, he has a specially long, 50-yard lead for him so that the dog, at least, can go 150 yards. A third told me that when he was caught in the street by an unexpected panic attack which brought him to his knees, he pretended to be deliberately crouching down, looking into a shop window.

One male agoraphobic, who was an area secretary in an agoraphobic organisation, said he got as many telephone calls from men as from women: 'Women will pour their hearts out, but the men aren't so trusting. They want to be sure what they say will not go beyond you. It's very hard for a man to admit he's got agoraphobia. People think it's pansy. If a man says he is frightened to walk down the road, he'll just be laughed at. Men have got to earn a living and even though they're probably going through sheer bloody hell, they won't admit to it.'

This particular man is a washing-machine mechanic. As he was completely housebound with agoraphobia, he solved his financial problems by having a telephone installed out in his yard, and doing his washing-machine repairs there ('It's my little prison'). None of the neighbours knows he has agoraphobia. 'I get them saying, "Aren't you going out? It's a lovely sunny day." I have to make some stupid excuse. It's the same for the kids on their open days at school. They say, " You won't be able to see my work." And they nag me about holidays, of course, but I can't manage them.' He has now had agoraphobia for some five years, the first attack coming without any warning: 'It came at a quarter past eight in the morning, out of the blue. I got palpitations. I thought I was dying. I said to the wife, quick, get a doctor. The doctor made things worse by telling me to have a week's rest. If he had said, "Get out of the bloody bed, there's nothing wrong with you," I'd have snapped out of it.'

But a sceptical attitude like that does not always work. Another man, who had had panic attacks ever since his schooldays, failed to improve despite his father's accusations of laziness. He had left school at sixteen and started work as an electrician's mate. He was getting panic sensations once or twice a day, and on one of these occasions he fell off some machinery and had to leave his job. His panic states increased at his next job and he had difficulty in working at all. 'My doctor prescribed tranquillisers. I took these, but did not notice any difference. Due to this and time off sick, I got the sack. This time it was happening a lot, when walking home from work and so on, so I refused to go out of the house at all. This went on for a year. I signed on the dole, and used to hire a taxi to go down there to get my money and go back in it, too. My father was getting very agitated by then, thinking I was lazy, and couldn't get to the bottom of it. He went with me to my doctor and the doctor recommended I went to a psychiatrist. I agreed and spent about an hour with one. He just said that as far as he was concerned, there was nothing wrong. "My advice to you is to go and get married." I was then about eighteen. He was very sharp and abrupt. So my father took a firm stand and said if I didn't go to work, he would throw me out, it was plain laziness.'

The result of this was that he used to say he had been out for jobs when he had not. This went on for six months and he then began to find it difficult even to go out into the garden. His father grew more and more anxious and annoyed and so he went to the doctor again, who arranged for him to be an in-patient in a psychiatric hospital. His father took him in his car and he had two fainting turns on the way there. He had a physical examination on arrival and after three days saw the psychiatrist, who questioned him on his past life. He saw the psychiatrist once a week, and meanwhile stayed in the dormitory and persuaded another man to get sandwiches for him. The psychiatrist told him to find someone, preferably female, and try and get out with her at least twice a day, even if only for the distance of one yard. He was to get a few sweets and suck those. Gradually he went from one yard to ten, then managed a quarter of a mile by walking a few yards behind someone. After that, he had to practise going alone to the pub and try to increase the length of time he stayed there. The hospital had a private bus service and he would get on a bus with a companion, get off after one stop and walk back with her. He would then go two or three stops; and finally could manage the nearest town. He was introduced to trains, on the same principle, until he went out for the day. This method continued, increasing distance all the time, with coaches, buses and going into cafés. At the end of three months he was allowed to go home.

Although his improvement was sufficient for him to get a job, he still had to hire a car to get there, as he found he could not cope with the trains after all. This was expensive, so he approached several people at work asking if any could give him a permanent lift. He did not tell them why, believing his boss would think him crazy. One night he left at 5 p.m. and took two hours to get home. He telephoned a friend at every phone box he came to, and she talked him home.

By doing his shopping locally, he has now improved – aided by his girlfriend, who goes on buses and walks with him. 'If need be, I can get to work and return on my own, but I would find it difficult – particularly in the evening when the traffic is building up. I don't take tranquillisers; but I would like to improve. I think to myself, well, when the time comes to marry, and if my wife gets sick, I will have to carry on. This bothers me from the man's point of view.'

This situation actually happened to another male agoraphobic, whose wife had developed multiple sclerosis. 'My wife finds it extremely difficult to shop,' he said, 'and would also like to see her relatives on the other side of London, but she can't go alone, and I can't take her. At present, her sister helps with the shopping and I help in the house.' This man's agoraphobia came on suddenly, after two months of marriage. 'When the doctor came I was in no condition to answer any questions coherently and he told me it was some kind of nervous or mental condition. But this I couldn't accept, as I was convinced it was something physical. One tends to have an image of people who suffer from mental conditions, and I did not think I was like that.' After further attacks, he signed off work for ten weeks; but although he finally returned six months later, he became incapacitated by more attacks and could not leave the house. Gradually the symptoms reduced in intensity and for the next six or seven years he could manage to get out by car, although he was reluctant to go anywhere by foot, and had a fear of public transport. During that time he had a lot of personal and domestic difficulties and his condition deteriorated again.

He then attended group therapy for a number of years at a nearby psychiatric hospital, until the group folded. 'This period convinced me that one has to find out the cause of it. I rather object to the mechanical, behavioural ways of cure, of inducing panic. Perhaps I have adjusted and adapted to the situation to the extent that I have not actively sought out new forms of treatment. I have not a great deal of confidence that it could be effective. I gave up teaching about two years ago, and run a tiny garden centre from my front garden. In a sense, I'm more contented than when I was working. It's surprising how friendly one seems to get with visitors.'

Phobics undoubtedly have an instinctive feeling about treatment, as in this last man's case. The more persevering ones will shop around until they find a therapist whom they trust, or a treatment to which they feel they can respond. Some may prefer the analytic approach, which considers the phobia to be a defence against anxiety, a symptom of underlying, unconscious conflict. The analyst's aim is to find the cause of this conflict, often hidden in the subconscious since childhood. Others may prefer behaviour therapy treatment, where the approach differs radically: the behaviourist considers that the specific fear has been 'learned' and therefore it is possible to 'unlearn' or 're-learn' it. *Why* it has been learned is not, therefore, the focal point; instead the patient is encouraged to overcome his fear by relearning to tolerate the feared situation or object. The emphasis is on getting the person to behave in a different way; to try out different practical solutions to the problem. (Details of techniques are given in chapter 12.)

In psychiatric clinics at hospital, behavioural methods are rather more likely to be in use. What still varies in these hospitals, however, is whether single or group treatment is more successful. Research is still being carried out on this – although there are obvious economic advantages in having one therapist managing a group of agoraphobics rather than just one individual. In this area, experiments are going on regarding the training of nurses to take over groups of phobics, under direction.

At the Institute for Behavior Therapy in New York, an agoraphobic is never put into a group immediately as, according to Dr Barry Lubetkin, 'There are lots of things they may need to work out in private therapy and, for many, a group setting may be too overwhelming. Eventually, 60 to 70 per cent of the individual agoraphobics are placed in one of our groups. In the groups, we use the "buddy" woman system. Patients go out and practise things together: a woman who is afraid of crossing wide streets goes out with a woman who is afraid of going upstairs.'

Dr Charlotte Zitrin, who heads the phobia clinic at the Jewish-Hillside Medical Center, Long Island, New York, also finds the group method very supportive – although individual sessions are also given. The weekly group sessions last from three to five hours, and continue for ten weeks. The patients – almost all women – first meet at the hospital. Together with a therapist, they walk away from the hospital, then go into a store in the neighbourhood, then into buses and trains, and finally into Manhattan – generally the most frightening thing for them. Some patients are given Imipramine, an anti-depressant that helps curb panic attacks: others are given a placebo (a standard method of measuring the effectiveness of medication). So far, there has been a 91 per cent success rate with patients treated with Imipramine and therapy, and a 71 per cent success rate for those treated with placebo and therapy. Of those treated, 80 per cent have remained improved.

Dr Zitrin estimates that six out of every 1,000 people are agoraphobic, and has found that some 50 per cent of agoraphobics have a history of early separation anxiety – such as being afraid to leave their mother to visit friends. She has also found that Jewish and Italian women – whose families tend to be close-knit – are more often agoraphobic than women from other ethnic groups. So far, over 80 people have been treated at the Medical Center, under a four-year research programme into agoraphobia.

For the last four years, Brian Wijesinghe, Principal Psychologist at Claybury Hospital, Woodford Green, Essex, has found that the best results have come from a combined approach of group and behaviour therapy. He conducts a two-hour session. During the first hour, the agoraphobics can bring up whatever problems they want to talk about. And in this first hour, he also gets them to think of the possibility of their problem being a symptom of underlying conflict – an escape route, where to be ill is the only way out. One woman, for instance, developed agoraphobia when her husband started to have an affair with a neighbour – this being a way of expressing her feelings. During the second hour, Brian Wijesinghe uses group hypnosis, or standard relaxation techniques, to relax them. Then, having set each person a target for that day, he gets them, individually, to carry it out in imagination. This is then followed by the person doing it in real life.

With one group he found that, as they progressed, they started to talk about their lives at home and their marital upsets. He then discovered that some of the husbands had become very depressed, through not knowing what was going on in the group; so they were invited to come along. After that, they understood what was happening and it helped create a balance in the marital relationship. Brian Wijesinghe has now started to mix groups – such as female agoraphobics and male travel phobics – and has also found this to be successful. He finds, with agoraphobics, that the simple behaviour therapy approach of learning to overcome difficulties only scratches the surface, and that the patients were resistant to this. 'In nine out of ten cases,' he said, 'the problem stems from difficulties in relationships, and it was that which made me turn to the group approach. The group also gets strength from working together.' He does not have a fixed method of treatment, considering it important to vary the approach, according to the patient's needs.

Dr Julian Hafner carried out an experiment at Maudsley Hospital, London, into whether individual or group treatment was better. Both the group (numbering 41) and individuals (16) had, in all, four days' treatment. Dr Hafner found that individual treatment was harder for the patient. Four dropped out of the individual treatment, whereas none of the group dropped out.

Discussion was a vital part in group treatment. 'The way they talked was astonishing,' said Dr Hafner. 'Almost from the moment they were introduced, they would talk and talk. They were over-joyed to be with people who understood. The power of being able to share with other people who had suffered for years was over-whelming. Three women, brought along by their husbands, hadn't been out of their homes for years. So many people had thought them stupid or sick. How, they said, could you explain you are all right on a bus if sitting down, but that you will fall if you stand? Laughter was infectious, too. One fat woman described how, farcically, during a panic attack, she had rushed out of a shop and nearly knocked a little girl over – and the whole group laughed at the scene for nearly a minute. Friendships were made within the group, which resulted in patients going out together for meals, spending weekends together and so on, which was helpful in reinforcing treatment.'

The first afternoon of treatment was crucial, for both group and individual. There could, with the group, have been a mass panic, but fortunately there was none. 'Walking was the trickiest thing,' said Dr Hafner. 'A lot were convinced that they were going to fall or faint – and you can't convince them that they won't. One woman insisted she couldn't walk more than 50 yards without collapsing; another wanted a syringe to be available, and I had to keep one in my pocket. But walking never turned out to be quite the problem they expected, as the other patients reassured them.

'I suggested they used various techniques, such as starting by going up and down on their toes and then giving a series of small hops. I explained if they could do that, their legs could take two to three times their weight. If patients thought they were wobbling, or drawn to the right side, they were afraid other people would think they were drunk. I would get them to walk along a line and get another patient to try and pull them off. On the first day of treatment, I got them to feel they *could* walk, and would gradually be able to manage being on their own. So they learnt to walk with intervals of space between them. I found that if I invited patients to say what they wanted to do, it was better than if I tried to push them.

'On the second day, they went in pairs into buses and stores and into Hyde Park. On the third and fourth day, they went to places like the Crystal Palace, and I got them to walk in open spaces, on their own if possible. We went on the underground and although a few of them feared this, and stiffened, they allowed the group pressures and my pressure to get them on it.' (They reverted to avoiding it once treatment was over.)

Dr Hafner saw all patients 2 days after the treatment, then at intervals of 3 months, 6 months and 1 year. They were told to telephone if they got into trouble, but they rarely did. At the end of 6 months, patients' improvement level remained the same as it was after 4 days. In all, 55 per cent of the group improved, as against 48 per cent of the individuals. Some patients in the group, and in individual treatment, were given tranquillisers; but although these reduced panic attacks, there was no real difference in outcome between those who took them and those who did not. Those who had, however, had really not had the real experience of being exposed to their fear, so when the treatment was over, they were less able to cope.

'I had the feeling that those patients who relapsed after treatment had marital problems,' said Dr Hafner. 'I saw the husbands with their wives whenever possible, to give them the opportunity to listen to their wives talking. Sometimes I felt that the husbands were weaker: one or two admitted that they were so frightened their wife would leave if she improved, that they would rather she remain an agoraphobic. Some husbands are over-possessive.'

He feels that exposure to the fear in reality is much more effective than doing so in imagination only: 'I have been struck, after an imagination session, how often the phobics are still afraid of going out and feel they are walking oddly.' This is where other patients in a group can be reassuring. 'Whatever patients say about each other,' says Dr Hafner, 'is more potent than what is said by a doctor. I suspect this is because doctors had promised in the past to get them better. The universal remark made to me by patients was that they had been let down by doctors, so it's important to say that you'll *try* to help, rather than you *will* do so.'

On the whole, general practitioners come under severe and often justifiable criticism from agoraphobics, who complain that their doctor dismisses their sensations as 'nerves' and automatically prescribes tranquillisers. On the other hand, agoraphobics tend to present their sensations as 'symptoms' and doctors seem to accept this rather than explaining the sensations are usually due to an over-reacting nervous system. In an article in *The Practitioner*, Dr David Julier warns doctors that: 'The agoraphobic patient may make heavy demands on the sympathy and perseverance of the practitioner; his capacity to maintain a supportive relationship can make a crucial difference. Exasperation at the patient's dependence or the spouse's complacency can lead to hostile "interpretations" about her manipulative conduct, which are rarely helpful, and the physician should aim at an attitude of equanimity and encouragement.'

Dr Julier stresses that the patient should be told that this problem is shared by some 300,000 others in this country; that he or she is not going mad; and that the panic symptoms are not physically harmful and sooner or later should recede. Although he sensibly suggests that any sources of stress – like marital trouble or difficulties with children or housing – should be tackled, it is hard to see quite who is to mastermind this. The doctors themselves have not the time. He does, however, give some useful practical suggestions that doctors can pass on to patients: 'Many patients are helped by using a stick, pram, shopping-bag on wheels, or a dog; they are less anxious in the dark or with an overcast sky, or when wearing dark glasses and sucking strongly flavoured sweets. They should be urged to use a bicycle, moped or car and to have a telephone at home; and to tell a number of friends about their phobia so as to establish a series of "safe" places along essential routes.' Mild tranquillisers, he believes, are useful, along with certain anti-depressants. He also thinks it is feasible to train nurses, health visitors, social workers, or even a relative to carry out a programme of graduated activities, on behaviour therapy lines, of exposing the patient to the feared situation – which should be supervised and controlled by the GP.

It is up to the family doctor to decide whether to refer the agoraphobic for psychiatric assistance – although this assistance is not always available. One teaching hospital in London had, at one stage, to close its waiting list for those wanting behaviour treatment, as there were too many patients for the psychiatrists and psychologists to see.

For this reason, there is a growing involvement of psychiatric nurses in more responsible roles. At Maudsley Hospital, for instance, a scheme has been set up to train nurses to administer psychological treatment. It is anticipated that most of their patients will be out-patients. Some of the treatment will be carried out in the patient's own home, so it is likely they will work from bases such as day centres. They will have to be supervised by informed psychiatrists and psychologists who, through these nurses, will be able to reach far more people than their time at present allows. Already many nurses help out on the routine side – taking groups of agoraphobics out, for instance, and then reporting back – and this has been immensely time-saving.

Most of the agoraphobics I contacted relied heavily on tran-quillisers or anti-depressants and – sometimes literally – took two steps forward and one back, depending on their home circum-stances. Those in their forties and fifties mostly got the standard explanation from the doctor that it was due to the menopause. But although the menopause can bring on upsetting physical sensations, and may indeed aggravate agoraphobia, it is not the cause. Unfor-tunately, women who are told this tend not to look further for treatment. Some doctors also come up with the have-a-baby pre-scription. Ironically, in some ways, having a baby *does* help. Many said that pushing a pram gave them a feeling of great support and comfort. But then so, for that matter, does taking a dog for a walk.

Having confidence in the person treating them plays an important part in recovery, particularly as agoraphobics tend to be pessimistic about getting better, rather than optimistic. 'When I first went to see a psychiatrist,' said one women, 'I did not like him at all; in fact he was almost rude to me. But I think this was done to eliminate the "*malade imaginaire*", as it is obviously very difficult to assess the extent of the illness at first consultation. I did not have deep analysis but we had weekly meetings for three or four years, when we discussed my problems and he gradually built up a new confidence in me.' This lack of confidence was stressed by quite a few, often after a marriage had begun to falter, or husbands stopped making love to their wives.

If the kind of treatment the phobic is having does not work, knowing there *are* other kinds is very helpful and can stop a lot of despair. In one case, a woman who had been attending a hospital psychiatric clinic said: 'The analytic treatment I was given there was absolutely useless. In fact, I got worse and began to analyse other people as well as myself. Eventually, after reading about behaviour therapy, I asked if this was available, but they didn't even know what I was talking about.' This attitude is not confined to England. One British woman, now living in Canada, said: 'For a year I underwent pure Freudian analysis. I discovered things about myself, my attitudes to my mother – living in England – and my father, who died years ago. After the year was up, I still had panic attacks, still could not walk alone unless accompanied, still the dreads, the alarms and excursions.' She shopped around for other treatment, as so many phobics are forced to do, in ignorance of what is available. 'We always feel that someone has the panacea, the magic answer that will wash the stupid, idiotic, predictable fears away. Many will-o'-the-wisps do we chase. Will hypnosis do it? How about an acupuncturist? Finally, an article on behaviour therapy. For me, this is obviously the answer . . . but there is not one practising behaviour therapist here in this town.'

In their hunt for a cure, some phobics try spiritual healing. One agoraphobic who tried this found it very soothing. 'It was a relief to go somewhere where I did not have to say how I felt. Just talking about my symptoms made me feel bad. I wanted to be healed and was quite content to sit there. The healer just said, " You don't have to tell me, I will find out." She would put her hands on me and it was as if she was looking in my head. She would always give me some exercises to do, like ones to strengthen my spine and relax my head and shoulders to take away tension in my head; and she would give advice – like saying I was a perfectionist and took too many worries on my shoulders. I just kept going and I noticed so many gradual changes, like finding I was able to visit people and go to the pictures. I felt calmer; something was guiding me into the right way of doing things.'

When I went along to the same house of healing myself, into the public room, there was an undeniable air of tranquillity; healers sat, for some half hour or so, with their hands on the patients, giving them their entire concentration. The atmosphere was entirely different from a busy doctor's waiting room.

Rather alarmingly, a number of phobics have electro-convulsive therapy on the advice of their psychiatrist without, it seems, any true understanding of this treatment. Indeed, one phobic said that 'after three electric shock treatments, I began to feel that if my nerves could stand that, then they weren't too bad and I discharged myself.' But most people seem to have a blind faith in whatever is prescribed for them – even to the extent of minor brain surgery. Several phobics stressed that this surgery had been successful, but the fact remains that they had very little knowledge of precisely what had been done and why.

Even being a voluntary patient in a psychiatric hospital can have a deleterious effect. After one such unsuccessful spell, a middle-aged woman said: 'Now I feel so hopeless and can only hope that the day will come when more is done for people, instead of putting them into these dreadful mental hospitals, where you are made to feel like an imbecile or, at the least, a neurotic nuisance.'

Depression figures largely in the lives of agoraphobics and some strong anti-depressants have an immediate and successful effect.

Most of those who take them, even if previously housebound, are able to face going out quite confidently. But one phobic spoke for many when she said: 'This anti-depressant drug was very effective. From being completely housebound, in a few months I was able to go out shopping alone, felt on top of the world, and that I could tackle anything. Thinking myself quite cured, I stopped taking the drug and within six months was back to square one. My doctor has put me back on it again, but it just isn't having the same effect. Now, of course, I am afraid I am hooked on drugs, and so I have a double problem.'

Another woman, also taking a powerful anti-depressant, found that with its help she can face going to town and using the motorway. But she is still terrified of long journeys, especially where a traffic jam may be involved, and now feels she can never be completely cured. Her fear had begun originally when driving to work and getting constantly caught in traffic queues: 'I began to dread these jams. I'd feel cold at the sight of the end of the queue and quite often would find I wanted to use the toilet, which of course was impossible. Within four or five months, I found this was happening at traffic lights as well.'

Her fear of incontinence is widely shared and usually stems from an incident where a person has a sudden urge to go to the lavatory, is not near one, and gets a panic attack. The next time she goes out, it either happens again, or she thinks it will happen. One women could only manage a journey by car if she was sitting on a bucket all the way, with a blanket around her, because her husband used to get angry at constantly having to stop the car for her. Others will not even risk going as far as the local shops.

At a group meeting of people with various phobias which I went to in New York, a young man admitted to this fear. He said that one psychiatrist suggested that he went ahead and wet himself in public, and confronted his fear. 'I tried it on the beach,' he said, 'but it didn't cure me: I just felt ashamed.' What was helpful to him, however, was the immediate admission by another phobic that she had the same fear. All the phobics present found it useful to talk about their fears, their progress or lack of it, and their methods of coping.

Many sufferers develop their own strategies for coping with, even curing, agoraphobia, which are usually commonsense – and often on precisely the same lines, unbeknown to them, that they would follow under many psychiatrists. 'I started trying to cure myself', said one women, 'by first going just inside a large store, and walking around near the door for a while. Then when it was a quiet shopping time, I went in a bit further, then a bit further; until one day I walked straight through the store, in the front and out at the back. I didn't stop, but just kept going. Finally I found I could go into a large store, and even stop and look around.'

Dr Claire Weekes's books, *Self Help for your Nerves* and *Peace from Nervous Suffering*, and her long-playing records, are also of great do-it-yourself value to agoraphobics. Dr Weekes recognises that the major drawback to treatment, as far as agoraphobics are concerned, is that they cannot leave the house to get it and have to rely on a relation or friend to drive them, which is not always possible. Dr Weekes's basic technique is to explain the causes of agoraphobia; reassure phobics that their symptoms are not unique; and give suggestions as to how they should cope with their panic. In *A Practical Treatment of Agoraphobia* in the *British Medical Journal*, Dr Weekes wrote: 'In my opinion, dependence on constant medication to tranquillise nervous symptoms or on learning how to avoid having them – for example, avoiding waiting in a queue – carried the danger of leaving the patient vulnerable to the return of the symptoms at any time ... A patient must be taught to cope with his symptoms. If a technique needs a name, perhaps mine could be called "coping through understanding".'

Undoubtedly a vast number of agoraphobics progress after the relief of understanding that their panic attacks stem from over-anxiety and stress. 'But why didn't anyone tell me this before?' is the general reaction. This underlines how important it is for GPs to explain these panic attacks to agoraphobics. Tranquillisers may well be needed, too; but the panic attacks will get more and more incapacitating if the agoraphobic does not understand them or have ways of coping with them.

It was because there was such a lack of understanding, and help, for agoraphobics that the two main organisations in the phobic field came into existence; the Open Door, and the Phobics Society.

The Open Door, run by Alice Neville, an ex-agoraphobic, started in 1965 after a huge response to a radio broadcast she made about agoraphobia. Mrs Neville retired in 1975 and the organisation – now a registered charity, under the name of The Open Door Association – is being run by Mona Woodford. It is a self-help organisation and information service for agoraphobics. Newsletters are sent out to members and there are over 40 area secretaries throughout Britain, who act as contact points for local members. Mona Woodford herself holds a weekly meeting for agoraphobics at her home at which a consultant, known to the group, comes along to give treatment. Meetings are kept friendly and informal as she feels that otherwise the agoraphobic would never make the tremendous effort it requires to get there.

The Phobics Society was started by Katharine Fisher, also an ex-agoraphobic. Once cured, by her own self-help methods, she began to hold self-help meetings in her home to help other sufferers in her area. There was a wide response, meetings were held elsewhere in Britain, and in 1971 the society was registered as a national charity. Its aims are to promote the relief and rehabilitation of all phobics. Self-help papers are sent to each member on joining, and these include suggestions for agoraphobics on how to alleviate anxiety as well as information on how the condition starts. Newsletters are sent out; and Katharine Fisher's aim is to set up centres where phobics can go for help. She runs the head office of the society from her home and has area organisers – many of whom receive council grants – in various parts of Britain, who run group meetings. Members are encouraged to meet and set up their own self-help groups.

I myself came across a number of ex-agoraphobics who had similarly started a local group, and achieved a great deal. One woman, for instance, who runs a Surrey group, persuaded the Medical Officer of Health to let her use the local clinic for her group, and arranged for a psychiatrist to attend and give advice. Another, in south London, hired a hall after her house grew too small to hold all the members and has a psychiatrist from a nearby hospital coming in voluntarily to give advice. Her husband goes out by car to collect agoraphobics who are housebound.

Agoraphobia is the most disabling phobia of all. In the case of those who are housebound, it has become a way of life, an accepted condition. This pattern can be hard to change – particularly if there are other complicating factors such as family relationships, severe depression and any other neuroses which may require psychiatric help. But it is mainly up to the agoraphobic as to whether or not she takes steps to improve. Those who have had the courage to be collected and taken to one of these groups have found this has at least helped to overcome their deep feeling of isolation.

There is always the danger that they will just sit and swap 'symptoms' and feel worse; but it allows them to establish comrade-ship and a rapport with others who have time to listen to them – which doctors do not. As my own doctor said: 'What *can* you do? You have a waiting room full of patients, and you ask what their symptoms are, and they say, "Now doctor, let me tell you in my own way." But there just isn't the time for this.'

Self-help groups can provide an outlet for this need to unburden one's problems. Perhaps they are the agoraphobics' own answer to some of their needs.

2

Spiders and Insects

'Sometimes she is the admired heroine deserving of reverence, at times the recipient of men's souls after death, and at other times the villain who induces fear, abhorrence and sinister forebodings.' (From *The World of Spiders* by W. S. Bristowe.)

Spiders, for their size, provoke a surprising amount of dislike. Superstitious rhymes abound, though mostly in the spider's favour: 'If you wish to live and thrive, Let a spider run alive'; and 'Kill a spider, bad luck yours will be, Until of flies you've swatted 53.' Another superstition is that they are venomous. Shakespeare, in *Richard II*, wrote: 'But let thy spiders, that suck up thy venom . . .' And during the examination into Sir Thomas Overbury's murder, a witness claimed the countess wished him to get the strongest poison that he could, and he therefore brought seven great spiders. Indeed, the Anglo-Saxon name of 'attercop' for spider meant 'poison-head'.

As well as breeding superstition, spiders were also credited with various medicinal virtues. A common country cure for jaundice was to swallow a large live house spider, wrapped up in butter; a similar remedy was given for ague in Ireland. A recommended cure for fever was to wear a spider in a nutshell round the neck; and in a fever case in 1760, a doctor recommended that the patient 'eat a spider, gently bruised and wrapped up in a raisin or spread upon bread and butter'.

In *The Folklore of East Anglia*, Enid Porter says that one remedy for whooping cough was to hold a spider over the patient's head and say, 'Spider as you waste away, Whooping cough no longer stay.' After this, the spider was put in a bag and hung up until it was dead. Again, spiders were used to counter rheumatism and ague, either by being eaten alive or by being carried around in a box until they died, when they were replaced by new ones. Cobwebs were also used as a cure – placed between two slices of apple. And until quite recently there were recorded cases of East Anglians using handfuls of cobwebs to stop cuts from bleeding.

Spiders were also reputed to bring luck. A story told about Frederick the Great was that one day, when he was about to drink a cup of chocolate, he left it for a moment to fetch his handkerchief and on his return found a large spider had fallen from the ceiling into the cup. He rang for more chocolate, then heard the sound of a pistol shot. The cook, having been persuaded to poison the chocolate, believed himself discovered, and had shot himself. In another legend, a spider was said to have woven a web in front of the cave where Mohammed was hiding, convincing his would-be captors he could not be inside.

Other countries share similarly superstitious attitudes. The Hausa tribes of West Africa treat spiders as folk-tale heroes because of their superior wisdom; the Bhils and Mats of India worship them as the recipients of ancestral spirits; the Chibdas of Central America do likewise, believing that rafts of spiders' webs are required to cross a river on the way to the centre of the earth; and the Teton Indians of North America treat them with considerable caution in case ill-treatment is avenged by other spiders.

Present-day European attitudes are less romantic. In 1948, for example, in a court case in Norwich, a judge ruled that the defendant had insufficient reason for charging out of the hotel without paying the bill, after spotting a couple of spiders on the bedroom ceiling.

Many people mildly dislike spiders, but a phobic has a much more intense reaction. 'Seeing a spider,' said one, 'makes me rigid with fear; hot, trembling and dizzy. I have occasionally vomited and once fainted in order to escape from the situation. These symptoms last three or four days after seeing a spider. Realistic pictures can cause the same effect, especially if I inadvertently place my hand on one.'

Other descriptions include: 'My tummy drops, I occasionally pass water; my heart beat increases tremendously, I sweat, and while the spider keeps still I am unable to move. If the spider moves, I am galvanised into action, but am not really aware of where I am going'; and, 'If a spider starts to run towards me, I am petrified with fear and unable to move out of the way. I just stand there sobbing and shaking and the colour drains out of my face, leaving me white and haggard looking.' Shock is present, too. 'I feel rather cold and distant and get the sensation common to any bad fright, which in my case is that the head isn't joined to the body'; and, 'Recently I came downstairs early in the morning and walked into a spider hanging on a long web. The spider actually touched my face and in my fear I tore at my face, scratching it in several places, became hysterical and was very nearly sick.'

Fear of spiders usually has its onset in early childhood and is rarely strong enough to be carried through into adult life. The fear can sometimes be related to a specific childhood incident; but there is no known reason why this should continue after puberty. Almost all spider phobics are women and few, if any, additional phobias are involved. In a study of animal and insect phobics (22 women: 1 man) carried out at the Maudsley Hospital by Isaac Marks in 1966, the family background of patients seemed stable, without many phobias, though half the cases were fearful as children.

Out of approximately 300 replies to a letter I wrote in *Woman* asking phobics to contact me, 26 were from spider phobics. All but 3 said the phobia had begun in childhood, before the age of 10; and 15 related it to a specific, remembered, incident. Some thought they had 'caught' the phobia (usually from their mothers). A few, now mothers themselves, were afraid they would, in turn, transfer their fear to their children – which had already happened in a few cases.

The childhood incident which had set the phobia off was usually slight:

'I can remember when it started. I was about six years old, just going to sleep with my light on, when I suddenly saw a large spider going across the ceiling. I called downstairs for someone to come and kill it. My dad came up to see what I wanted and when he saw it was just a spider, he laughed and got hold of it by its legs and dangled it in front of my face. I just froze, really thinking he was going to drop it in my bed and from that moment I have been petrified of spiders.'

Another phobic said her first recollection was when she was about three or four, playing in the garden, and got 'caught' in a web in some flowers and thought she was stuck there, like a fly. She screamed for her mother as there was a spider crawling towards her up the web. The phobia got worse in adolescence and, when studying biology at school, she had to ask for a note from home to excuse her from going to any lessons about them.

A fear of spiders set in, with one woman, at the age of six, when she was bitten by a largish but ordinary black house spider. This gave her a very swollen finger and a slightly inflamed arm. Then a comic ran a series on man-eating spiders – and she developed a near-hysterical fear of spiders.

Several phobics had experiences of other children placing real or imitation spiders on them, or having encountered them unexpectedly. One remembered feeling a strange sensation when she put on her sock, and discovered a spider curled up between her toes. Several times after that, her clothes had to be removed to convince her that she was 'clean'.

A few mentioned that they also dreamt of spiders. 'As a child', said one, 'I had nightmares of spiders as big as houses all coming down the street and trying to get under the doors.' Another housewife said she'd read that spiders are symbols for sex in dreams and nightmares, and admitted that when she had nightmares of them, she was sexually aroused at the time. As a child, she could never understand where their 'bones' were, or their mouths, and her mother told her not to ask – just as she did about sex.

Dreams are considered important in psychoanalysis as, in theory, they can provide a short cut to understanding the feelings and urges that the patient has been repressing. Discovering these, and discussing them with the patient, can therefore help relieve the anxiety which may have led to a phobia. In *Dreams and Nightmares*, J. A. Hadfield cites a case of orgasmic nightmare, involving crabs and horrific spiders, occurring after a boy took refuge in masturbation after failing to get affection from his mother. The creatures, in this dream, represented physical sexual sensations: the crab personifying the gripping feeling caused by abdominal contractions, and the spider 'with its soft squashy body', the post-orgasmic sensations.

Sexual symbolism in the case of spiders has been rife since the early days of psychoanalysis. Karl Abraham, in 1922, considered the fear of spiders symbolised the unconscious fear of bisexual genitalia ('the penis embedded in the female genitals'); and Melitta Sperling, in the *Journal of the American Psychoanalytic Association* in 1971, said that 'Most investigators seem to agree that the spider is a representation of the dangerous (orally devouring and anally castrating) mother, and that the main problem of these patients seems to centre around their sexual identification and bisexuality.' In a laconic comment on these views, in his book *The Meanings of Fear*, Stanley Rachman writes: 'It is worth pointing out that, even if Abraham and his successors are entirely correct in their assumption that a fear of spiders is symbolic of a fear of bisexual genitalia and/or of a phallic, wicked mother, there is room for optimism . . . fears of bisexual genitalia and wicked mothers are capable of being desensitised readily and quickly.'

Behaviour therapy, with the use of desensitisation, has certainly proved a successful way of treating specific phobias like this. Precise methods of treatment naturally differ, but the usual one is of relaxation (sometimes by use of drugs) combined with the patient imagining the object he fears, then actually experiencing it. In one case quoted in *New Horizons in Psychology*, the patient was first asked to rate the characteristics of spiders that caused her most anxiety. These turned out to be: size (the bigger, the worse); colour (the 'blacker' the spider, the greater the fear); hairiness (the more hairy, the more anxiety); movement (the more active, the worse it was); and proximity (the closer, the more fear.)

At the start of the treatment, the patient was asked to think of these characteristics, in ascending order of anxiety. In order to associate pleasurable feelings with the presence of spiders, the patient was played some music she liked at each stage of the treatment. Finally, still in a state of relaxation, real spiders were presented. At the end of the course, the patient was able to handle very large house spiders with complete ease.

In ten cases of specific phobias successfully treated by J. P. Watson, R. Gaind and I. M. Marks, three of these were spider phobics. One concerned a twenty-three-year-old secretary, with a long-standing phobia which prevented her from visiting a country cottage now available to her; the second was a forty-year-old woman who had reached the point of being unable to open a window in case a spider appeared; and the third was her nineteen-year-old son who wanted treatment after striking a colleague who showed him a spider among some wood.

The patients had both fantasy and practice sessions. Each fantasy session consisted of the patient listening to tape-recorded scenes which described them entering a situation built around spiders, and suffering disastrous consequences (the situation was based on the patient's particular fears of spiders, already discussed with the therapist). As well as describing the situation itself, the tapes also described the patient's reaction, their physical and mental state. Four themes were used: each lasted six to seven minutes and each was played four times. The total 'playing time' was therefore nearly two hours.

In practice sessions, the patients were encouraged to approach an assortment of spiders, and deterred from avoiding them. The therapist's attempts to provoke anxiety were gradually abandoned, as patients seemed to get over their phobic avoidance more quickly if therapists did not add to their anxiety.

Each patient was asked at the end of the treatment, and at subsequent follow-up interviews, how many marks out of ten he would give himself. The last rating obtained was, on average, 7·8 and patients were all delighted with the result.

Another case, reported by David Julier in *The Practitioner*, in 1973, concerned a twenty-one-year-old teacher, who had been phobic about spiders since, at the age of eight, she was accidentally shut in the lavatory with one. At the same age, a member of her family made sexual advances to her. At nineteen she married and moved into an old, spider-ridden house. Her fear of seeing a spider now dominated her, and she took outpatient treatment. This consisted of six sessions of listening to frightening stories of spiders for thirty minutes at a time, followed by six sessions when she was encouraged to handle spiders. She made fast progress and at the end was able to organise a school project with real and model spiders. At a six-months' follow-up, she still had no symptoms.

Although the sex complications in that particular case were ignored in treatment, sometimes a psychiatrist will combine brief 'insight' psychotherapy with behaviour therapy. In other words, he will discuss symptoms with patients and try to make them see what they stand for. In an example of this given by Dr Joyce Emerson in her booklet, *Phobias*, a patient sought treatment for her spider phobia after she, too, had moved into a new house with a lot of spiders. The patient was quoted as saying: 'I was so depressed I didn't know what to do. The doctor told me I was focusing my other fears on spiders and I came to realise I was afraid of sex. I also disliked my mother for her coldness – I think she was afraid of sex too and had transmitted her fear to me. The doctor told me to imagine a spider on a ledge near me, then a bigger one, and nearer. Then he managed to get hold of a plastic spider and put it close to me. All the time I was completely relaxed by the injection. Now (six months later) I find I'm much better. Most of my fear has vanished and I've altered my opinion about sex, though I'm still cold towards it.'

Knowing the reason behind the phobia, even if sexual, doesn't necessarily cure it without treatment. A woman who is now seventy recalls walking to school with some friends, and stopping to look at a large spider in its web. As she did so, she was suddenly aware of a man behind a hedge exposing himself to her. She understood how her disgust transferred itself to spiders, but still cannot overcome

In another case, however, a person's phobia did improve after she worked out for herself that a very stressful time in her childhood, when her mother was in a sanatorium, coincided with her being taken to see the film of *Swiss Family Robinson*, in which a tarantula bites one of the boys. A further case of personal stress being transferred to the phobic object was cited by a young student: 'I am sure this is linked to my parents' separation when I was fifteen. My mother and I left our large country house and moved to a small town flat. Here unusually large spiders nested in the attic and this aspect of my new home became linked with my distress at my father's rejection of me.' She decided to take treatment when she found her spider phobia was affecting her way of life. It prevented her from going anywhere new; gave her nightmares; and began to affect her work. After a 9-month course of behaviour therapy treatment, she has learnt how to relax and can now calm down within hours — rather than days — of seeing a spider.

It is usually only when a spider phobia makes life impossible that treatment is sought. The reason for *not* getting treatment is invariably the same: 'It seems an impossible thing to ask any help for and I could imagine my doctor's comments if I did'; and, 'I simply did not know where to go and also I would have felt so stupid.' Some phobics resort to self-treatment: 'I tell myself that there's going to be a spider in the bath, sink, and so on, so when there actually *is*, it isn't so much of a shock.' A fifteen-year-old schoolgirl said she had tried to get rid of this fear by reading everything she could find about spiders: their life history and all the facts and figures on how they live. But it did not help. She found herself confronted by a motionless spider in the bath one day, controlled herself and tried to approach it and pick it up, but she could not manage it. One useful line of defence in these circumstances is taken by a woman who wears contact lenses. She carefully peers into the bath before putting them on, and if she sees an unfocused blurry black blob, she washes it down the plughole without 'seeing' it.

It is, however, surprising that more people don't try to get treatment, considering the minor havoc this phobia can create in their lives — a havoc unappreciated by the non-phobic. In one instance, a housewife has to stay watching a spider all day, until her husband comes home, in case it moves and she 'loses' it. If she *does* lose it, 'I go out and leave everything, even if the house is in a complete tip.' Recently, when she was waiting for her baby to finish his breakfast, she put the paper down and saw a big spider running up her body: 'I jumped up and screamed. I couldn't touch it, so I found myself jumping up and down until it had gone. I changed my clothes, got the baby and caught a bus straight down to my husband's work where I burst out crying.'

An equally distraught reaction came from another housewife, who dreaded going into cupboards or corners when doing her housework, and constantly scanned rooms in other people's houses. She claimed she could 'sense' a spider and this 'sensing' was mentioned by other phobics – one of whom said she could often 'feel' if there was a spider in the room and could not settle until it was found and destroyed. It is no good someone merely putting it outside, because she remains on edge – convinced it will return and probably bring its mate with it. And a teenager claimed that she could tell, on going into a room, not only if a spider was present, but if it was 'looking at her'.

All this causes the phobic to spend a lot of time checking such things as baths, washbasins and door edges. At least ten minutes a night was spent by one teenager in inspecting her bedroom, behind the headboard and under the bed ('The thought of it actually being in the bed is terrible'). It also prevents one woman from putting her hands into any hidden corners; doing any gardening; sitting on grass. When going anywhere new, like a hotel, she has to spend the first few hours 'enemy hunting'.

The idea that a spider is actually lying in wait may seem ridiculous to a non-phobic, but phobics themselves often feel strongly that, somehow, the spider has managed to take the offensive. 'They seem sinister to me,' claimed one woman, 'and somehow I feel they *want* to frighten me.' Many feel that spiders make straight at them, ignoring others in the room. But the 'sinister' side was constantly reiterated, along with their repulsive appearance and, no matter how small, the 'threat' they posed. In one or two cases, phobics mentioned that people can take on spider's characteristics ('predatory and sinister'). When one woman was trying to extricate herself from a relationship, she said the other person took on spider-like attributes: 'I felt I was being caught, made a victim and sucked dry.' A Jamaican woman looked nervously around as she talked to me, and said, 'You shouldn't talk about spiders, they don't like it', recalling that the African 'Ananci' figure, who was half-man, half-spider, was a crafty and cunning individual. For many they seemed to personify malevolence, even evil, personally directed at them. 'They're unnatural,' said one. 'They're too humanoid: they do things that other insects don't do, and behave more like human beings. There's a sort of calculation: laying the trap and waiting – particularly in a country that has very few predators.'

The spider's habit of being able to drop on *you* without warning was also feared. This point was made by a man who had developed a spider phobia when a young boy in the country. 'They can be behind you,' he said, 'descend from the ceiling on a strand, or gallop out from under. They always seem to come towards you. Some don't make webs but spin a sort of lateral thread along the top of the window, and run along that, as a nasty balancing act. I feel this is another part of the plot: they think to themselves, "Humans expect round webs, so let's give them *this*".' The man concerned thought his phobia was passed on to him by his mother ('She was once alone with a spider in a room, and tried to kill it with a flat-iron: but spiders know if you don't like them, and it moved three inches to the left and *defied* her').

He himself thought the movement was the most horrifying thing about spiders. 'When one starts to move, however small, I stop. One takes such precautions that they don't touch you: that's the ultimate horror. I used to think the hairy ones were worse until I was in a house with one which looked as if it was made out of one continuous piece of black skin.'

In this case, the man's childhood fears were reinforced by films and books. He remembers the Saturday morning film sessions including a character called 'The Spider Woman' who was dressed in svelte black satin on a throne, with an eight 'legged' web behind, two being her arms. There was a period in his childhood when he believed they ate people and no amount of reading persuaded him otherwise. He also felt that spiders didn't die. He remembers a semi-witchcraft film called *Night of the Eagle*, in which the heroine keeps an enormous dead African spider in an eighteenth-century pill box. Her husband throws it into the fire and the scene ends with them going to bed while, out of the ashes, comes the spider. Now, some 30 years later, this man can still be paralysed by a spider which is big enough and takes him by surprise.

The titillating fear that a spider can bring is often deliberately exploited in films, when tarantulas are invariably falling on the heroine of the day, and on book covers – particularly paperbacks – where spiders decorate books on subjects from VD to murder. (And are never touched by spider phobics, whatever the subject.)

Less easy to understand, perhaps, than a spider phobia is the similar fear some people feel on seeing moths and butterflies. An American college girl, for example, said she could sense their presence before seeing or hearing them. 'The sound of their wings fluttering away terrifies me, and their erratic flight heightens my terror. This condition worsens if I am aware that we are in a closed room: I invariably attract the moth, and as it flutters around me, beating its wings relentlessly, I become so frightened that I literally cannot move.'

She used to live on Long Island, which is a relatively humid area where moths are abundant in summer, being brown with about a 2-inch wing-span. At night, she would often wake up, having sensed a moth in her room: 'Sure enough, I would hear the wings flutter and see the almost hyperactive insanity of the creature. I instinctively would tie my hair in a knot as, being over three foot long, it seemed to attract moths. I couldn't leave the room to call someone to get rid of the moth, for fear that I would be assaulted by it on the way to the door. So I would secure the sheet over my head so that no edge could serve as an entrance for the moth.'

During the summer she cases every room before she enters, to make sure no moths are in it. She has also had her room painted completely in white, so that she can spot a moth quickly if it comes. 'I fail to see how a feathery little creature could hurt or harm me, but when one comes near all my logical arguments disappear and my panic reservoir opens.'

Similar feelings were expressed by other women in England. 'I go cold if one is anywhere near me, especially in confined spaces like toilets,' said one. 'The local pub where my husband and I go still has an outside toilet and of course the light always attracts moths. When I go to this pub in July and August, I would rather burst than use the loo, unless someone goes in first and kills everything. I can't kill them, you see; I have this fear that when I put my hand near they will land on me, which is even worse.' She dreads going to bed in case one has flown in during the day and is lying in wait till she puts on the light.

One mother said that her seventeen-year-old son had had a phobia about moths ever since he was twelve months old – when apparently he was watching a television comedy show which had a very large butterfly which kept landing on one of the comedians. To this day he completely loses control of himself if a butterfly or moth comes near him. On sunny days he always stays indoors as much as possible.

Some phobics find moths almost too repellent to kill and have even injured themselves in attempts to get away from them. Dr Emerson, in her booklet *Phobias*, mentions a woman who fell off her bicycle when dodging large butterflies zooming across her path; and who, another time, picked up a screwed-up piece of brown paper from a shelf, only to find it was really a large, dead brown moth. Through shock, she fell off the chair on which she was standing and sprained her ankle. She also has to leave both buses and underground trains when moths or butterflies get in – claiming strongly that this actually happens.

Phobias about flying insects seem more intense, in some ways, than those about crawling ones. Wasps, bees – even daddy-longlegs – seem, to the phobic, to be an enemy that's always coming at them. The one advantage is that they are mostly around for only three months of the year. 'But those three months seem like an eternity to me,' said one sufferer. 'I am always on the alert and the slightest buzz from a wasp sets me off sweating and panicking. I rush out of the room; or sometimes right out of the house. The pans could be on fire and dinner burnt to a cinder, but I would not go back in until my husband returned and removed the offending insect.' Before going into the bathroom she gets her husband to inspect it, close the window and spray fly-killer around. Then, if nothing appears, she ventures in, but her husband has to be within earshot in case of emergency.

One would expect a fear of wasps to stem from having been stung by one at some time; but this is not necessarily so. Indeed, one phobic who has been stung several times says it's not the pain that she minds, it's the thought of them being around her head. Another housewife admitted that she'd never been stung: 'But if I see a wasp, even in the distance, while out in the open air, I go hot and then cold and clammy, scream or cry uncontrollably – frightening my two children or anyone near, who think I am having a fit. Fruit shops are taboo; three summers ago I passed one and the wasps came within a few feet of me. I threw my shopping into the road, along with my purse, and ran. People stared at me as though I was mad and picked up the fallen articles and returned them to my husband who, red-faced, was trying to apologise and explain.'

Her husband begs her to sit in the garden with him and, after years in a flat without a garden, she can understand his joy in it – but she still refuses and sits in the kitchen with a can of fly spray near by. Outings during the summer to the country, swimming lidos and picnics are a nightmare to her and she avoids them. 'I am only twenty-six, and the thought of this for the rest of my life is terrible. My husband understands my fear, but is annoyed that I am making the children, aged four and five, afraid of all flying insects.'

Dr Emerson's booklet also mentions a case of a thirteen-year-old girl to whom wasps were a symbol of violence. For her, feelings of violence were taboo – as were feelings of violence against her mother, who had neglected her. Her psychiatrist explained: 'The important thing for me was realising that her way of dealing with wasps was the way she dealt with any kind of fear. She felt compelled to run away from it.'

In *The Meanings of Fear*, Stanley Rachman describes the similar reaction of a boy of seven, brought in for treatment, who had suffered such an intense fear of bees for several years that he would run blindly away from them and had twice run across busy streets to avoid one. He would go white and tremble and sweat when confronted with a bee. He couldn't play out of doors in the summer, and had to go to school by car during both spring and summer terms.

The reason the boy gave for his fear was that, although he had not been stung himself, he knew several people who had been, or who were, excessively afraid of bees. He was treated, firstly, by being shown small photographs of bees. He was then helped to progress through different stages. These started with him being shown large photographs of bees; then coloured photographs; then bees in a bottle at the far end of the room; then dead bees in a bottle which was brought gradually closer; then a bee out of the bottle; then a dead bee on a coat; then several dead bees – and finally a session where he played imaginative games with these. After eight sessions, the boy was greatly improved, and his physical reactions to bees were much reduced. He was able to play in the garden happily and a long-term follow-up showed that the phobia had not returned.

There is naturally little sympathy for people suffering from phobias of such tiny creatures. The phobics themselves are only too aware of this; and indeed this realisation can sometimes help them during treatment. A. F. Fazio, in a report on treatment of insect phobics, found that having discussions with them about the harmlessness of an insect, and how much their fears are shared by others, caused a far bigger reduction in their phobic behaviour than when their treatment consisted of being actually confronted with insects.

But knowledge of an insect's harmlessness can't always overcome the panic they can cause. In the summer of 1975, for instance, a young man 'died of fear' after being stung. He had a phobia about insects and, according to the pathologist, mistook a twinge of pain in his chest (caused by an unusual heart condition) for a wasp sting. His fear was so acute that the action of his heart became genuinely upset and he died. This is obviously an exceptional case; but it shows non-phobics – who may dismiss fear of such small creatures as a joke – the depth that the fear can reach.

3
Fear of Flying and Heights

In the summer of 1974, an American woman hid for two days at Heathrow airport, rather than catch her flight to New York. When she was questioned by a police officer, she confessed to being too afraid to fly. She was allowed to stay another night at Heathrow and, next day, got as far as boarding a plane – but officials decided she was unfit to travel and she was taken to hospital.

Most people admit to nervousness about flying – apparent in the number of drinks ordered at take-off and the relieved smiles on landing. A real phobic, however, cannot fly at all. And fear can set in without the person concerned ever having flown. An Austrian woman, for instance, explained the onset of her phobia like this: 'I was about seventeen years old and had been invited to fly with a friend in his own plane, piloted by his pilot, to a weekend in the Austrian countryside. When I asked permission for this trip from my parents, they refused to let me go for several reasons. My friend and his pilot invited somebody else and the plane crashed, with the guest and the pilot killed. My friend got away with serious injuries. As soon as he recovered he flew again, crashed and was found dead in the wreckage.'

Her fear of flying took on such dimensions that when she could have escaped from Austria by plane to Italy, like most of her friends in the first few days of Hitler's invasion, she was the only one to stay behind. Eventually, she did get away, but by train and ship: 'To me, a plane is always identical with a flying coffin.'

More often, however, normal nervousness is hardened into a phobia about flying after a bad experience in the air. One woman who, as a child, had always been a keen plane spotter, said that she had looked forward for years to her first flight in a small plane. But she became scared stiff of falling as the plane banked, and thought the wind buffeting the sides of the craft would make it disintegrate.

Her fear was compounded on her next flight, a year after, on a regular airline: 'We got on board and then there was the take-off. There it was again, that horrible feeling as we gathered speed. It was creeping over me again, that old feeling of panic. I kept seeing everyone as puppets, all strapped to their seats with no control over their destinies, me included. Every time the plane did a variation of speed, or route, my heart would leap and I would hurriedly ask what was happening. When the plane started to lose height, I was terrified that we were about to crash . . . when we approached Gatwick airport, we were confronted by thick fog and all the planes at the airport had been grounded. The pilot came over the tannoy and informed us that he was going to try for a landing. Several times we swooped through the murk and then rose above it. We circled round for ages going up and down like a yo-yo. The plane vibrated and shook very loudly every time we ploughed through the fog . . . we had to get down because the fuel situation was getting desperate. We ploughed through the clouds once more, the aircraft buffeted about by the turbulence. We made a fairly heavy landing and the engines were immediately reversed to slow down the plane and I thought the damn thing had blown up. To make it worse, I looked out of the window and saw fire tenders pulling along beside us.'

It is often a bad take-off or landing which triggers off fear, though other aspects of flying can also do so. One phobic said that she dreaded the clouds ('there is no way out'), and another that she was terrified to look out of the window ('the thought of five miles of nothing between us and the ground is horrible.'). An ex-foreign legionnaire, who was so phobic about flying that his fellow legionnaires never told him they were due to fly until the morning prior to take-off ('I would have deserted'), said his latent fears had turned into a phobia after he had flown in some really rough aeroplanes around the desert, helping another legionnaire to deliver vegetables to different camps. 'This pilot, his face was all burnt, he'd been in a crash himself. He'd get on the plane and he was always drunk, and he'd start peeling bits of rubber off it ("This thing's falling to pieces, all rotting," he'd say). He'd keep bits of wire and screw-drivers in his pocket. Then he'd take off with such a jerk, I'd be on my back with potatoes all over me.'

What this man particularly feared about flying was the lack of control that a passenger has. As with claustrophobia, this and the feeling of being closed in are the two chief fears. When I pointed out that, as a passenger, he was equally without control in a car or train, he said that at least he could fling himself out: 'But in a plane you have at least five minutes after it starts going down when you can't do a thing about it. In a car or a train, what's more, you don't know anything about it: it's over. In a plane you could sit for ages and listen to the screaming and shouting as it plunged down.'

Many suffer from this over-imaginative, mental picture of impending disaster. One twenty-two-year-old girl said that waiting for her flight to be called was like the last few minutes before execution. On take-off, she feels it is only her own supreme effort of will that gets the plane off the ground and her continued concentration that keeps it airborne. Consequently, she is rigid throughout the flight. If an air hostess hurries into the cockpit, she is convinced something is wrong. 'The noise of the engines is another horror, because you wait to hear them splutter and stop.'

Some phobics trustfully seek reassurance from fear of the plane crashing by asking their therapist if he will 'guarantee' their safety. Dr Leon Salzman, Clinical Professor of Psychiatry, Albert Einstein College of Medicine in New York, told me that he knew of one psychiatrist who, in answer to the pleas of his aerophobe patients, would give them a signed pass saying, 'I hereby guarantee that this plane will arrive safely at its destination.' Dr Salzman himself is careful not to give anybody anything in writing. However, he

reassures his patients that the flight they are afraid to go on has every
reason to arrive – just like the previous ones. He feels in this connection that phobics are naïve. Statistically, plane travel is safer than
going by car (and indeed when one pilot was asked what he considered the most dangerous part of flying, he replied, 'The drive to
the airport'). But statistics do not stand up against the phobic's inner
conviction that the plane he is going on will crash.

One phobic admitted that her fear is not confined to the thought
of just being in a plane. She even panics on hearing a plane flying
overhead, being convinced its engines will fail and it will crash
down on her house. One night she was so carried away by this fear
that, hearing a plane passing overhead while having a bath, she
leapt out and dried and dressed, thinking that at least they
would find her body clothed when they dragged her out of the
rubble.

Her fear, she thought, may have started when she was about six
years old, and was playing in the garden with some friends in a small
tent. The friends were teasing her and would not let her out of this
tent. While struggling to do so, she heard a plane flying particularly
low overhead and thought it might have been coming down: she
panicked and screamed until she was released. There were no
immediate after-effects, but when she was sixteen she started going
with a boy whose home was near the scene of an air crash, and it was
at that age that she began to feel serious fear.

Some phobics think they can manage to fly but balk at the last
moment. One woman, in fact, had twice refused to get on a plane
after having arrived at the airport, under the absolute conviction
that it would be her last journey. A young professional woman
agreed with her: 'I am certain I am going to die; it's unshakeable. I
just feel slightly incredulous when I don't.' She used to become
depressed about ten days before a flight and started sleeping badly.
Two nights beforehand, she would be very sick – not helped by
heavy drinking to overcome her fears: 'On the day I was flying, I'd
no sooner hear the whine of the aeroplane, the diesel fumes, than
I'd start grovelling in my handbag for pills. Even seeing people
off, I'd get incredibly over-anxious, just hearing the sounds of take-

off. I'd avidly read details of any plane crashes, too, though I'm usually not interested in such things.'

Her phobia had begun after she had made 23 flights in 3 months, on her way back from Australia to London. ('On flight 4, I was crying on landing; by flight 10 I was drinking; and by flight 16 I was talking gibberish. I ended by taking some incredibly strong drugs and knocking myself out.') She was, at the time, engaged to a man who was working in Italy, despite her father's opposition, and she felt guilt as well as fear over her – now rare – flights to see him. On one of these flights, she had a very bad touch down, and at that point stopped flying.

As this hampered her job, she went for treatment at a London hospital. On her visit, the therapist explained the desensitisation technique he would use. It involved his drawing up a list of the situations which frightened her about flying. He would then start off with the least frightening, ask her to imagine it, and then get her to relax. She would go on imagining the same scene until she was no longer frightened, before the next most fearful situation was presented to her. To find out what situations she most feared in flying, the therapist asked her to think about the scenes he was going to describe to her and then rate them from 0 to 10. She rated gently cruising along as nought, and take-off as ten.

At her first practice session, she carried out relaxing exercises and learnt how to switch her mind over from imagining a pleasant scene to making it empty. Sessions then continued twice weekly, with a different fear situation being tackled at each one. She found that, as these were described time and again, the fear they raised almost disappeared. It was then suggested that as her anxiety over the whole scale was now minimal, she took an actual flight. Although she had to have tranquillisers and a drink at take-off, her anxiety at the airport and on the plane was decidedly less than usual. She still avoids flights if she can, but at least can fly if she has to.

One disadvantage about treatment relying on imagery and relaxation is that the patient might think himself ready to fly when lying relaxed on a couch far away from the airport, and then find, when it came to reality, that this was far from the case. Indeed, this happened once when one woman felt cured enough to fly to the Middle East – but not sufficiently cured to fly back again. Dr Robert Sharpe, of the Centre for Behavioural Psychotherapy, London, always takes his flying phobics up in a plane – either on a regular scheduled airline flight or in a Piper Cherokee four-seater belonging to the London School of Flying – and claims a success rate in the high 90 per cent range.

Leslie Solyom and colleagues compared four different treatments for fear of flying:

1 *Systematic desensitisation.* For four one-hour sessions, relaxed subjects imagined flight scenes in ascending order of anxiety; then, in four more sessions, they repeatedly watched a film on flying with scenes at the airport and take-off and landing.

2 *Aversion relief.* Each subject had to write (in the first person, present tense) and then record on tape accounts of past flying experiences, including the situations that made him anxious, like roaring engines, and his responses. Subjects then heard their own tapes through loud-speakers. 20-second silences were interspersed before the anxiety-provoking situations and responses, and followed by a finger electric shock. In the next sessions, the flight film was used with the same shock treatment, as follows: Scene of the stewardess walking down aisle – 20 seconds – electric shock, button pressed (feeling of relief); sound *Fasten your seat belts* – 20 seconds – electric shock, button pressed (feeling of relief), *bumpy weather ahead* . . .

3 *Habituation.* Same procedure as with aversion relief, but without shocks.

4 *Group psychotherapy.* Patients discussed their phobia and other neurotic difficulties, then met an experienced pilot at the airport, who spoke about air safety, pilot training, and so on.

At the end of the treatment, there was a general test flight. The first three behaviour therapy techniques all significantly reduced air travel phobia; group psychotherapy, on the other hand, showed little success. However, it had an incubation effect, and at a follow-up some months later had caught up with the others.

Films have also been used successfully in treatment by Myron Denholz. In one study, using 18 male and 84 female volunteers, 160 twenty-second flight scenes were prepared – half of which were expected to provoke anxiety. For example: 'A plane is seen gathering speed for take-off. This fades into a scene of people inside the cabin. The background jet noise reduces and a dubbed-in voice says, "Imagine yourself on this plane as it takes off." The scene fades back to the plane which is seen to take off and ascend at an acute angle.' Appropriate sound-tracks were used, sometimes with instructions like: 'Imagine you are sitting in this plane which has just passed through some turbulence.'

The second group of 80 scenes were made deliberately pleasurable with, for instance, sound tracks with soothing music and commentary. Tape-recorded instructions in muscle relaxation had been given to all subjects prior to viewing. Groups of six to ten subjects, over three sessions, were shown one anxiety reel (27 scenes) and one pleasure reel (27 scenes) at each session. The final film version combined the 27 overall most pleasurable scenes, plus 27 scenes ranked in order of intensity of fear. This method had an 80 per cent success rate and it has been suggested that a library of such treatment films might be developed.

An airline itself co-operated with one phobic clinic in the state of New York. Ten patients there were on an 8-week course, led by Dr Manuel Zane, in White Plains Hospital. The reasons for their phobias differed widely: one man, for example, had been a pilot in the last war and had been unable to fly since. One woman had witnessed near catastrophe every time she was in a plane: once the plane in front had turned over on landing; another time she was in a near collision. A third patient had severe claustrophobia and had never been able to contemplate flying.

'First we had two group discussions at the hospital,' Dr Zane told me. 'Each patient had his own individual therapist, and we talked about their specific fears. Our next step was riding to the airport in little subgroups – six in a car, three therapists and three patients. When we got there, an Eastern Airlines pilot talked to the group and gave them factual information about flying. We then sat in an empty plane on the runway, which Eastern made available to us. The doors were closed and each therapist asked his patient what he was experiencing. Then there was a general discussion, so that they could learn what everyone else was feeling too. We then had another meeting at the hospital to talk things out for a day before an actual flight was fixed.'

The flight itself was a normal scheduled one; but Eastern Airlines had their senior pilot at La Guardia airport fly the plane. In addition, one of their captains, with 31 years of flying experience behind him, was with the group – who were mainly seated in the first-class section. Throughout the 35 minutes' flying time to Boston, the pilot kept up a running commentary over the tannoy, explaining what the various noises represented, as well as telling them the speed, altitude and other reassuring information. (Other passengers were merely told that the group was making its first flight.) All the patients managed the flight reasonably cheerfully: they reacted with a certain amount of fear, especially at take-off and landing, but it was *controlled* fear. One woman, for instance, as she felt herself becoming tense, realised that what she was actually doing was trying to stop the plane from taking off. Knowing this was impossible, she just concentrated on controlling her emotions. A second similar round-trip flight was made two weeks later.

Airlines in general may not lay on the red carpet treatment to this extent, but they all try to ensure that the atmosphere in a plane is as soothing as possible. (Unlike insurance companies, which tend to capitalise on aerophobia with advertisements like 'Will you leave anything you value behind when you next fly?'.) But on most planes there are relaxing in-flight films, piped music and drinks to order. Cabin staff, too, are trained to spot nervous passengers (not too difficult, as these are usually sweating or gripping the seat) and calm them. They are also taught to recognise passengers suffering from hyper-ventilation (over-breathing, caused by fear, which makes people dizzy or even unconscious) and cure it by getting them to breathe in and out into a paper bag. And as passengers are always scared by strange noises, like the undercarriage grinding into place, pilots are encouraged to explain these in advance. Most airlines carefully avoid the subject of aerophobia, but one broke the taboo in an advertisement addressed to its passengers as follows: 'Hey there! You with the sweat in your palms! It's about time an airline faced up to something: most people are scared wit-less of flying ... deep down inside, every time that big plane lifts off that runway, you wonder if this is it, right? You want to know something, fella? So does the pilot, deep down inside.' (Surprisingly, there was no drastic fall-off of passengers in response.)

Pilots certainly can develop a phobia about flying. Writing in *District Nursing*, Patrick J. O'Connor, consultant adviser in neuropsychiatry, Royal Air Force, said: 'In aircrew, the main complaint may be about suddenly flying into cloud, especially at night, or a feeling of being poised on a knife edge when flying at heights in excess of 30,000 feet where the horizon is below the pilot's comfortable gaze – the low horizon syndrome. Flight phobia in its fully developed form is a rare condition and probably does not occur more often than one patient in a thousand, but when it has developed it makes flying virtually impossible. In the case of the aviator, this may result in loss of his livelihood and I know of a number of men in the middle range of management who might well become directors but for their inability to fly.'

Phobics are only too aware of the disadvantages of not flying. 'I dreaded us going into the Common Market,' said one salesman. 'I knew it would mean me flying to Europe and of course it did. So I had to resign.' It also affects a great many people's holidays, forcing them to stay in their own country rather than go abroad. Quite a few come for treatment because of the marital discord and anxiety caused by one partner being phobic. 'Since my husband's promo-tion,' said one woman, 'he flies frequently and I feel the time must come when I'm invited to join him.' A few years ago, an American engineer called Nathan Cott worked out that his phobia had cost him more than a hundred thousand dollars of business. He put an advertisement in a paper, asking for other aerophobics to contact him, and received hundreds of replies. To cope, he organised the 'Fly without Fear' club. Members took part in group therapy, had reassuring talks with airport officials, desensitising sessions with psychiatrists and, after three months, a group flight. Now Nathan Cott flies round the world, lecturing on the subject,

One cheerfully vaunted theory is that fear of flying is linked to a fear of sex – the inside of the plane being the womb and the powerful engine thrust at lift-off being intercourse. However, many psychoanalysts feel that fear of flying is really a person's own private fear of being in a situation where they are not in control. Dr Leon Salzman says that, to him, 'Phobias are a very widespread and useful technique for dealing with a situation in which an individual feels he may lose control and not be able to manage. A person with a phobia of planes will drive to Florida, saying he is afraid to fly because of accidents. Yet he knows it is far more dangerous to go by car. So it's not an issue of danger; the issue is that in cars you are free and in control. A phobia is always symbolic: it's not the plane, that's just symbolic of a situation where you are under someone else's influence. The person who get a phobia is the person who will not take any risks, wants guaranteed safety. I deal with a person's need to control everything, and help a patient by saying that it's not human to be able to think that they can live in a world where they always have control. When they can accept this, the phobia disappears. Plane phobias are not based on previous incidents, but on previous anxieties. We didn't treat the pilots who refused to fly any more in the war as phobics.'

A fear of heights and of planes would seem natural stablemates – although one heights phobic said that plane trips did not worry her, because the ground was so far away that she could almost believe it was not there. But many heights phobics are terrified at being more than three feet above the ground, whether on a plane or just on some steep stairs. Montaigne commented on this fear in his *Essayes*: 'Let a Philosopher be put in a Cage made of small and thin-set iron wire, and hanged on the top of our Ladies Church steeple in Paris; he shall by evident reason, perceive that it is impossible he should fall downe out of it: yet can he not chuse (except he have beene brought up in the trade of Tilers or Thatchers) but the sight of that exceeding height must needs dazle his sight, and amaze or turne his senses ... Let a beame or planke be laid acrosse from one of those two Steeples to the other, as big, as thick, as strong, and as broad, as would suffice any man to walke safely upon it, there is no Philo-sophicall wisedome of so great resolution and constancie, that is able to encourage and perswade us to march upon it, as we would, were it below on the ground.'

Many heights phobics share a feeling of being drawn towards the edge. One said she cannot even look down from a high window without feeling physically weak, and had often wondered if she would be tempted to jump if she was on a cliff top. Another agreed with this Peter Pan urge to fly: 'It's a feeling that you are not subject to gravity, that you can move through the air without damaging yourself. The fear is not due to picturing what kind of injury you would get; it's the actual falling, not the result of it.' One woman who, for over ten years, has had a 'falling feeling' whenever there is a space in front of her, said: 'My advice to anyone else who has this phobia is to escape from the situation.'

Arthur Janov explains this reaction in his book, *The Primal Scream*: 'Somehow the neurotic must think that if he keeps things in control and "cooled" he won't have to be afraid any more. So the neurotic avoids what he fears – or what he thinks he fears. He stops flying and avoids heights. These activities often do help control these fears by isolating and compartmentalising them. But should a person come close to the *apparent* object of his fear, such as a high balcony with a low railing, what arises is the real fear which is symbolised by the current situation. The neurotic caught on this balcony may really fear loss of control over self-destructive feelings, not a simple fear of heights.'

Certainly the phobia can mask other kinds of fear. One therapist told me that she had just been treating a man who lived on one of the top floors of a high-rise block of flats. 'He came to us saying that his fear was such that he had to use his brother's flat on the ground floor. I got him up as far as the lift and I was convinced that his inability to get to his own flat was a wish not to have to face up to the sexual side of his marriage. His wife was overpoweringly attractive, and he'd somehow lost confidence in himself.'

A widow, whose fear of flights of steps, and even road kerbs, had begun after the death of her husband, was told by a psychiatrist that she had lost her 'prop' when her husband had died. And Karen Horney, in *Neurosis and Human Growth*, analysed a fear of falling as due to anxiety and insecurity: 'The phobia of falling from heights is a frequent expression of the dread of falling from heights of illusory grandeur. Consider the dream of a patient who had a phobia about heights. It occurred at a time when he had begun to doubt his established belief of unquestioned superiority. In the dream he was at the top of a mountain, but in danger of falling, and was climbing desperately to the ridge of the peak. "I cannot get any higher than I am," he said, "so all I have to do in life is to hold on to it." Consciously he referred to his social status, but in a deeper sense this "I cannot get any higher" also held true for his illusions about himself.' Dr Alexandra Symonds, Assistant Clinical Professor in Psychiatry at New York University College of Medicine, said that men often have phobias of heights. 'They are afraid they will fall, but it represents a certain unconscious wish to get up there.'

Phobics will usually only apply for treatment when the phobia is really affecting their lives. One man did so after his office had been transferred to a tower block. When he dictated, he normally strode around the room, but found he was unable to go anywhere near the window. He finally disliked even going into the room, and realised that without treatment he would have to resign. This treatment took the form of being taken up into higher and higher buildings, until finally he was able to master the Post Office Tower. By the end of the treatment he was able to go back to work without any difficulty.

A fear of heights is innate: babies, when crawling, will avoid going near the edge if they are on a table, or something higher, where they can see a drop. This natural caution can, on occasion, develop into a phobia after a frightening incident concerned with height. Even people who seem to seek out heights – like scaffolders – can sometimes become affected. 'You can sense their fear,' said a scaffolder I spoke to. 'They hand you things, but you notice they let you do most of the balancing work. I've known their nerve go completely and they can't even get down.' Had he ever had this feeling of panic? 'No,' he said. 'I *know* I won't fall.' In the same way – whether up in a plane, or on a bridge – phobics *know* they will.

4

Social Phobia

'My fear of people was strong enough to make me try and commit suicide,' said an eighteen-year-old girl.

This particular type of fear – commonly called 'social phobia' – is usually closely allied to a lack of confidence. It started, in this girl's case, when she left primary school and lost touch with all her friends except one. 'At secondary school I changed, especially when I became more aware that there was an opposite sex. I developed a fear of people in general, was frightened of making a fool of myself, always imagined everyone was talking about me behind my back, and worried what they thought of me. I became very self-conscious, with no confidence. I developed round shoulders, walked everywhere with my head bowed and seldom looked at people when I talked to them.

'I went to a grammar school where the boys were in one building, the girls in another, and we had separate playgrounds. I hated walking past their playground every morning and used to avoid doing so if I could – either by arriving late or using the back entrance. I never wanted to be picked as a form official and once I was "ill" on the first day of term so as to miss the elections. I wouldn't enter a room full of people on my own.

'Walking in the street was a nightmare. There was even a time when I'd walk on the opposite side of the road, if the bus stop I usually passed was crowded. Something I'll never forget is an argument I had with my father. He asked me to get him some cigarettes, and because I couldn't explain why I didn't want to go, we had a blazing row.

'I was a lot happier at college, but it was a trial for me encountering so many men face to face. Although I wasn't short of friends there, I didn't see any of them outside college. I didn't go anywhere – just sat listening to records, reading or writing letters. I knew that the only person who could help me was myself, but I was too nervous of people to make the effort.

'When I left college, I went to work as a shorthand typist in a small insurance broker's. I got the job through a friend's mother who recommended me, which saved me struggling through endless interviews. At that time there were only six of us working there, mainly elderly people, but it took me a long time to settle down. I trembled whenever the phone rang, jumped whenever a man walked past. I sat in my little back office all day pretending to be quite happy, but inside I was lonely and depressed. I daydreamed, thinking up situations I would like to be in. I convinced myself that I was just dumb, stupid, ignorant – a nobody. Gradually the firm began to expand, employing younger staff. My problems got worse – I wouldn't enter a room full of men, still hesitated at answering the phone. Then someone at the office held a party and although I worried all the week beforehand, and lost my appetite, I plucked up the courage to go.'

It was at this party that she managed to confide some of her worries to a male colleague, with whom she then fell in love. This did not work out and, despairing of ever forming relationships, she attempted suicide. Her boss then came to her rescue. 'I had a long talk to him and although I didn't tell him about my fear of people, I told him I was lonely and depressed, how I thought I was a nobody, could never have an interesting conversation, and that I couldn't take any more. He helped me more than anyone else just by listening and not telling me how silly I was. I think he really understood.

'Although I'm still very nervous of people inside, I've managed to hide it more now. I can confidently handle telephone calls, do counter work without blushing, laugh and joke with my colleagues.

My deportment has greatly improved. I look at people when talking to them and my speech, which used to be very rapid and stuttery, is now a lot slower and more precise. Although I'll be shaking like a leaf inside, I'll now enter an office full of men. I seldom go out, do not have a boyfriend, but this no longer worries me. My advice to anyone with the same phobia is to talk about it to someone.'

Unfortunately, many people with 'social phobia' find it quite impossible to do this. 'I never answer the phone,' said one such phobic, 'and if anyone comes to the door, I run and hide.' Dr Ian Falloon, who specialises in treating social inadequates at Maudsley Hospital, London, says that some of them cannot even talk to their own family, be in the same room as another person, or have any satisfactory sort of relationship. Because they find it difficult to talk and mix with people, they may end up by being housebound. However, they differ from agoraphobics, finding it *easy* to go out of the house alone and *hard* to go out accompanied by others. And, unlike agoraphobics, they get no solace from talking to mutual sufferers.

Social fears and anxieties do not always form separate entities like other phobias, but more often resemble agoraphobia in having a wider variety of symptoms. The term 'severe social anxiety' or 'social incompetence' may be more accurate than 'social phobia'. 'Social phobia' is often a combination of anxiety problems, a lack of social skills, and lack of self-esteem or confidence. The relative importance of each of these components may vary considerably in individual cases.

Symptoms of social phobia can include an inability to relate to other people at any sort of personal level, a fear of groups of people, an inability to talk in public, difficulty in looking people in the eye when speaking to them, anxiety about getting close to people physically or emotionally, inability to assert oneself and be positive, difficulty in expressing feelings openly, or putting oneself across confidently, often very clumsy gestures, a lack of ability to converse and difficulty in both starting off a conversation and keeping it flowing. (These fears are not always irrational, of course. Where does one draw the line between normal social anxiety, which we all have when we have to get up, say, and make a speech, and abnormal phobic anxiety?)

Social phobics have usually always had social difficulties. 'Often they are only children who have had an overprotected social up-bringing, and have not developed a sense of independence,' says Dr Falloon. 'They may be intelligent, but have never been able to use this to their best advantage, and can't function really adequately in an adult social role. It's usually most noticeable after they have left school and had to stand on their own feet at work, or university, and make their own relationships.'

Social phobia is one of the few phobias which affect more men than women. This is probably because although women may be just as socially anxious, they are able to exploit the woman's role and be demure and shy in a corner. Men, on the other hand, usually have to work and to mix. Being shy isn't 'masculine'. Men are therefore particularly conscious of, and upset by, their phobic reactions. One young man of twenty-six, with a fear of blushing, said: 'One aspect of this fear, and believe me it's a fear all right, is that you feel ashamed of admitting to anybody that you've got a problem like this.'

His phobia started when he was a small boy at school, and was brought out in front of the class and told off for some minor mis-demeanour. He still recalls the sense of public humiliation he felt and ever since then has had a fear of blushing. (A girl blushing is considered rather attractive and endearing, but when a man blushes it elicits jokey and sarcastic remarks from his male colleagues.) The fear of blushing made it hard for him to approach a girl and he also feels lonely because nobody else seems to realise what a fear like this is like. It affects his life in a number of ways. For instance, when he travels on any form of public transport, he has to buy a paper to 'read' on the journey – in a corner seat, if possible – as a kind of shield to make him feel more secure. He finds that when he's talking to people, he has to suck a sweet. As he doesn't smoke, it helps reassure him.

He watches television, on average, six hours every night. Television is, he finds, a medium which creates the illusion of social contact – without, in his case, the tension and anxiety that usually go with meeting people in a real-life situation. He reads a lot of American comic books, of the Superman variety – which is a retreat into a fantasy world, rather than taking up a more outward-going interest, like some kind of sport. For treatment, he has been to several hypnotists, but with no lasting results.

At Maudsley Hospital, a 10-week training course in social behaviour has been designed specifically to improve socially inadequate people. Groups of six to eight people take part, under the direction of a male and female co-leader. Weekly sessions last 75 minutes: 10 minutes is spent discussing the past week's activities; 60 minutes in demonstration and practice of difficult social situations, and 5 minutes in setting goals for the next week. A typical 10-week course would be on the following lines:

Session 1. Relaxation techniques; discussion of anxieties among the group; practice within the group of communicating with each other, such as shaking hands while looking each other in the eye.

Session 2: non-verbal expression. Gazing, touching, appearance, gesture; the group might act out picking up a person who has fallen in the street.

Session 3: vocal expression. This includes practising things like pushing through a crowd; saying 'excuse me'; and use of 'I beg your pardon', 'Would you mind repeating that' when unsure of sense of a conversation.

Session 4: simple verbal expression. Includes acting being at a cock-tail party, with members entering one by one and circulating from one small group to next; using 'ice-breaking' techniques such as comments on weather, or offer of cigarettes; expanding on 'yes' and 'no' replies.

Session 5: work situations. Includes conducting a job interview in front of group, with one member playing the boss and the other the applicant, and then reversing roles. Practising asking boss for time off; refusing boss's request to do extra work.

Session 6: expressing feelings. Includes taking a defective article back;

asking a person to move out of your way; queue jumping, with other members trying to stop it.

Session 7: group interaction. Members are encouraged to express any opinions and to participate as 'good listeners' in small groups; group rules are demonstrated, and speech-making is practised.

Session 8: initiating friendships. Includes starting conversations with member of same sex and opposite sex; arranging a future date; coping with rejection or backing out gracefully.

Session 9: sexual behaviour. Includes explicit teaching of sexual techniques and courting behaviour, including pop dancing.

Session 10: revision. Members suggest any other situations to practise.

Throughout the training programme, members are asked to keep a day-to-day diary of their social activity, as part of a self-help programme. In this diary, they enter their personal 'target situations' and give themselves points for the number of times each day they tackle them. Such targets might be 'Talking to secretary for five minutes'; 'Going for a drink with a workmate'; or 'Asking a girl for a date'. They then select five things they *enjoy* doing (such as watching television for 30 minutes) and reward themselves by doing one or more of these things if – and only if – they have amassed enough points from carrying out the difficult targets.

Social phobics seem to respond to treatment better in a group – where they can help each other to improve and relax together, as well as generally socialising and practising going into pubs, cinemas and restaurants. Members of the family, or close friends, often join in these activities, as it's considered important that they know about the treatment and understand it.

Ian Falloon describes the sessions as being 'a bit like a training talk before a football match. They provide a few special tactics and a lot of encouragement before the match.' But ultimately it is up to the members of the group, who *must* practise what they have learnt by going into the situation they fear.

One girl of twenty-eight carried out her own form of self-help with reasonable success. She had been very self-conscious about her hands, because when she got upset or worried they trembled, and sometimes shook quite a lot. She therefore didn't like giving to or accepting from strangers a drink or cup of tea or coffee. The first time this happened was when she was nineteen and was taken home by her boyfriend to meet his parents. Both this relationship, and a succeeding one, failed; and from then on she was conscious of her 'phobia'. She found her fears gradually spreading, and affecting her work as a secretary: 'At one time I found it difficult to take dictation, and type it back if it was given to me just before I was due to leave the office, or if the work was needed urgently and my boss was waiting for it; I would panic and my fingers would just seize up.'

She tackled her fears herself by taking her boss into her confidence, which helped a great deal. She also deliberately faced the situation by taking on an extra part-time job of typing phoned-in reports from news agencies. 'I really steeled myself to take on this job because in my full-time one I work alone and because of my phobia I have tended to isolate myself from social situations at work. When I go into the copytaking department for the first call, I feel rather nervous, but after that I am all right. I usually get one of the messengers to get me a coffee, so that problem is solved.'

She used to dread people coming into the office because she would have to offer them some refreshment and the more she thought about it the worse it became. Her boss was very kind about this and worked out a system that if more than one person came, she would hand round a tray. Initially, she couldn't offer anybody a drink that she did not know well, but this is lessening. She finds that if she thinks about it just before handing over the drink then she shakes; but there are people now to whom she will give a drink, so she considers things are improving slightly. She also used to dread being invited out for a drink from the office in case her hands shook, despite telling herself this didn't matter. She takes tranquillisers when she thinks she may face a 'difficult situation'. 'I know everybody has some dread of something, but people accept somebody who has an aversion to mice, or flies. If you don't like giving somebody a drink, though, they think you are anti-social and, if your hands shake, that you must either be "on the bottle" or a complete wreck. It's strange, really, as I strike everybody as a confident person; but with certain people, regardless of whether they are "ordinary" or "impressive", I become very self-conscious.'

She paid to see a psychologist privately, but he was of no real help: 'He said you couldn't attack the symptoms without dealing with the cause, and just put me on anti-depressant tablets. I think time is the only thing I have on my side.'

Another phobic, with a fear of eating in public, tried to cure herself. The phobia had started when she was in a restaurant and, for no reason, felt sick and sweated profusely when the food arrived. 'This then spread to eating food in other people's houses. If I knew the people well, I was OK, but if they were mere acquaintances, I could eat nothing. I usually felt panicky, because I knew it was insulting not to eat anything when my host had spent time and trouble preparing it. My family seemed to think I was being silly and no one took me seriously. So I tried to relax, breathe deeply and evenly, eat slowly and – what seemed most helpful – to take frequent sips of water with the meal. I now very rarely get these panicky attacks when eating out. I have trained my mind into believing that I am really hungry and this seems to work.'

One twenty-three-year-old, who also fears eating out, turns down almost all her invitations, with the result that she has very few social contacts. (Her fear, she thinks, stems from being over-plump as a teenager.) She says, sadly, that it's surprising how much of everyday life is centred around eating – such as meals in the canteen at work, dinner dates, holidays and so on. The last time she went on holiday was three years ago and it was virtually ruined for her. If she hadn't had some tranquillisers, things would have been a lot worse. As soon as she entered a restaurant or sat down to a meal with people not well known to her (by that she meant people other than her immediate family) she started to go hot and cold and her hands were usually wet with perspiration. As soon as she tried to eat anything, her hands shook uncontrollably. 'You can imagine how embarrassing this is, as people stare or laugh behind their hands at you, as if you're about to have some kind of fit.'

In another case, a married woman with three children finds it equally impossible to cope with her phobia. Yet her inability to talk to people for more than a short period has made her very lonely. 'I can't go to any activities or meetings or the children's school. I can't eat or drink out, and because of this phobia I haven't any friends and spend all my time on my own in the day. The worst part of it all is the flushed face and neck I get when I come up against one of these situations. If I could be cured of that, I am sure I would be over the worst hurdle.'

Talking to people with social phobia makes you very aware of their loneliness and curtailed lives. Yet strangely enough, sometimes only a gentle prodding is needed to help break the pattern of behaviour the phobia has established. A common way of treating patients who dread eating in restaurants, for instance, is for them to be taken to the hospital canteen when no one is there; then at the tail-end of lunchtime; and finally when the canteen is full. But the patient – or group of patients – needs a therapist to be with them, to help to calm their anxieties, for they are unlikely to have enough courage to try this out themselves.

One young man, who could not speak to girls without a panic reaction, was treated in this manner at a London teaching hospital (though when he saw his 'nurse/therapist' come in the door, he at first tried to dash out). It was several weeks before he would allow her to take him along to the nurses' dining room, when it was quiet. But once he'd been able to cope with the sight of women en masse, the nurse asked him over to her flat which she shared with five other girls. He was able to stay for an hour or so; and was so grateful about his improvement that he returned some weeks after that, on his own, to bring the flatmates some flowers.

In New York, a great deal of emphasis is placed on 'assertive training' – that is, giving people more confidence in social situations. Dr Lubetkin, of the Institute for Behavior Therapy, told me that, 'The emphasis for many people in New York is on getting out and finding a mate, and people are constantly pressured into seeking other people out. A lot of them have tremendous difficulties in doing this. People fear going into new groups to meet people for the first time; they fear sitting around in restaurants with their husband's associates; and they fear meeting the opposite sex. They say: I am afraid I am going to leave a poor impression on the others present; I don't want them to find out how insecure I really am; it would be awful if I wasn't approved of, if they didn't like me. We are often dealing with the way the patient thinks about himself, his feelings of worthlessness, and so on, and you've got to get him to challenge these myths he operates under.'

At the New York Institute for Behavior Therapy, the techniques practised are similar to those used at Maudsley Hospital in London. 'We have a number of therapists working with us,' said Dr Lubetkin. 'We find many social phobics lack a "problem solving" skill: they cannot deal with "power" situations such as how to ask for more salary; how to approach a professor after class. So we spend time teaching patients these skills; how to handle a boss who comes on very strong and starts yelling; how to disarm a boss's arguments; actual things you can say rather than apologise. They also need to know how to talk to a stranger and what to do when they meet someone in a "singles" club.

'Assertive training is often role playing, simulating social situations in the office and outside. After the therapists portray the scenes, they then switch roles, so that the watching patients can model themselves on them. We then bolster their repertoire, and give them new ways of responding to these situations. We talk about inflexion of voices and intonation. If they feel more confident, we have them go outside and we give them tests – such as stopping a stranger on the street for change.

'We also do "shame exercises", developed by Dr Albert Ellis, which help the patient to overcome inordinate fears of appearing foolish. The only way we can get them to challenge this idea is to get them doing things that *would* invite disapproval, such as yelling out loud the stops in the subway train, or speaking to strangers in a lift, and learning that they'll survive the discomfort. The point here is that we show the individual that all the awful things that he anticipates will occur when he is risking activities with unpredictable consequences, won't occur: that people are not that concerned about them, that they are not being watched and scrutinised. The only way to find out is by experience.'

Dr Lubetkin himself thinks that it is the more passive individual who is more prone to phobias, particularly those phobias which have 'secondary gains' – which conveniently prevent the phobic from getting into the situation he really fears. 'I treated a woman who had been a "stair phobic" for four years,' he said. 'She developed the phobia when she had to go to a dance and she was afraid no boy would ask her to partner him. So as she walked up the stairs to the dance hall, she started getting anxiety symptoms and then she maintained it as it prevented her from getting into socially difficult situations.'

As most of us, sooner or later, find ourselves in precisely the same situation of worrying about being a wallflower, or being socially unsuccessful, why do not far more people develop social fears? Dr Fensterheim, who runs assertive training sessions at his clinic at New York Hospital, thinks, in fact, that most people *do* need this training ('Who isn't shy? Who doesn't have trouble saying no to unreasonable requests? Who does like speaking in public?'). As for those who are affected intensely by social fears, after a reasonably trivial incident, he 'believes that there are people who have sensitive nervous systems: a little stimuli can set off a big reaction. With one group I had, I got them relaxed and I only had to start with the simple word "criticism" – criticism of American literature – and even that set off anxiety.'

Dr Fensterheim holds training groups for the psychiatrists and psychologists who will, in turn, be treating social phobics, and these are asked to carry out the same things they will be asking their patients to do – such as going into a restaurant, asking for a drink of water, and then leaving without tipping. (Understandably, most of them have almost as much difficulty doing this as their future patients.) Dr Fensterheim feels people are becoming increasingly afraid to antagonise other people by, say, challenging bad service. So patients might be asked to telephone to complain about their rubbish not being removed, or practise asking for change for dollar bills without buying anything.

Overwhelming fears of social situations can lead to specific fears like blushing, talking to people of the opposite sex, answering telephones or making speeches in public, taking any form of test or examination, and even fear of physical contact. One man, with a fear of being touched by women (which would have set Freud delightedly to work) travels on public transport with a rucksack on his shoulder, ready to ward off any women who approach within a foot of him.

There is one specific phobia that I came across quite frequently, and that is a fear of vomiting, or of seeing anyone else vomiting. Of the 300 or so replies from my letter in *Woman*, 35 were from 'social phobics' and 18 of these had a specific fear of vomiting.

One woman described her reactions this way: 'If I am on a bus where a person is behaving perfectly normally, but is very pale, then I am convinced that he is about to be sick and I have to get off the bus immediately. It is the same in any vehicle. If I should happen to be in a car after a party when one of the passengers had been drinking more than usual, then it is hopeless. I must get out, even if it means calling a cab which proves expensive and is, in other people's eyes, nonsensical. Once, when younger, a girlfriend felt very sick after a dance and as my father had to drive both of us home, it was all I could do not to scream hysterically. As it was, I had to be sedated when we eventually reached home. Also, two years ago on a flight to Yugoslavia, a girlfriend who was sitting beside me gradually got greener and greener until the hostess said, calmly, "You had better give her a bag". As soon as I realised what was going to happen, I warned the hostess of my likely reactions and the fact that I had actually been under a psychiatrist for treatment – not that he had helped. She said I would be perfectly all right, but she was wrong. My friend told me afterwards she had been sick three times and then felt much better. But I had my head between my knees and was – I am told – absolutely screaming, in spite of the tranquillisers I had taken in case of this eventuality. So I was the one who was embarrassingly led off the plane, helped by my friend. It appears to be something I just cannot overcome; no tablets help. It makes it very difficult for me to lead a normal life, as I am literally terrified even going to the office each day.'

Another woman, with the same fear, felt this was caused by her mother, who was rather obsessively concerned with keeping the house clean and had threatened to punish her children if they were sick in bed. As there were eight children, there seems no reason why only one should have reacted so strongly – although one other sister was affected to a lesser degree. The woman concerned is now fifty-three, and her life has been very constricted. She has always feared to be away from home, especially to sleep, and is wary of eating anything she feels unsure of. She has never gone on a boat or been abroad. 'I have swallowed thousands of tranquillisers and now have pills for high blood pressure, which I am sure is bound up with the phobia.'

A major worry for this woman was of being ill when she was pregnant and having to cope with her infant daughter when she, in turn, was sick. Another, newly married, woman shared her fear: 'The fact is', she said, 'that I feel I have only a few short years before my husband will want children, although he knows how I feel and is in sympathy with me. And I want children, but I want to get rid of this fear and all the added fears that go with it. I am desperate to find a cure, or at least to come to real terms with it. Being sick can't be as bad as all that, otherwise everyone would be scared of it'.

Another young girl is reluctant even to get married, faced with the thought of pregnancy and morning sickness. She has no idea why her phobia started, but can remember that when she was seven, and her youngest brother was sick, she jumped straight out of an open window. Her school life was marginally affected as she had to have a seat next to the door so that she could run out if anyone was sick and was excused biology lessons as the diagrams she had to study affected her. 'I would even give away my dearest possession to someone who was feeling sick to try and take their mind off it. On one occasion I gave away my pet hamster.' She attended a child guidance clinic, but they could do nothing about the phobia; nor did she have any better luck later on in her teens. 'I went into a psychiatric hospital, where they injected a drug and I talked very freely, but still no cause was found. I have had hypnosis, drip treatment and E.C.T., but nothing has cured my phobia.'

A twenty-three-year-old student – who, strangely, was more afraid of women vomiting than men – had never sought any treatment because she was rather ashamed of her phobia. Another woman thought the one thing that would cure her would be to have children of her own – believing that she could never leave her own child when it was sick – only to find that she could and did.

'The first person ever to show me any kind of understanding to my problem was a woman doctor,' said one phobic. 'She made me realise that having a phobia doesn't make you end up dotty.' Her experience at a London teaching hospital wasn't so fortunate. 'I had to fill in a stupid questionnaire with questions like, "Do you enjoy sex more now, less now, or the same, since you had your phobia?" I mean, what the hell's that to do with throwing up? Eventually I was put on some secret white pills and was told I would feel fantastic after three or four days. Nothing happened. I felt drugged and became really neurotic. I had a jab of pentathol, which made me cry, and got me nowhere. The psychiatrist said he could find no reason why my phobia persisted. My God, ten visits to a hospital, just to be told that.'

Many of those with a vomiting phobia could recall the incident when it first took hold, but it did little to help them, and none of the phobics I was in touch with myself had been successfully treated. Most of them had not even tried. Brian Wijesinghe, Principal Psychologist at Claybury Hospital in Essex, did, however, treat a vomiting phobia successfully. The twenty-four-year-old woman concerned had had this phobia for 11 years, but it had worsened in the 18 months prior to seeking help and was greatly restricting her activities.

The patient was, at first, asked to imagine being on a crowded underground train (a very threatening situation for her), and then to think of the following anxiety-evoking situations, one at a time: 'You are on the platform of an underground tube station – standing inside a crowded train – feeling hot and becoming increasingly apprehensive – the train suddenly stopping inside the tunnel – heart beating fast – surrounded by people – tightness in the throat – hand trembling – stomach turning over – legs feeling weak –

feeling sick in the pit of the stomach – hearing someone retching – vomiting yourself – unable to escape from the situation.'

This situation did not, in fact, make the patient anxious, because she could not hold the image for long and, even when she did, it was not vivid. So she was then trained to enter a hypnotic trance. In this, she was able to visualise the tube journey vividly and showed obvious discomfort. This was maintained by asking her to describe her visual and emotional experiences at regular intervals. After 80 minutes, with the image still remaining clear, her anxiety started to subside. When she was brought out of the trance she said that she could think of the tube journey without feeling threatened by it. A later test under hypnosis showed her still free of anxiety; and a follow-up a year later confirmed the success of this treatment. Hypnosis seemed to have a two-fold effect: lowering the patient's anxiety, so that she faced up to the fear without switching off; and making her realise that she was not completely in control during the imaginary scene, which accentuated her emotions.

Severe social anxiety – including specific anxieties like a fear of vomiting – can lead to severe depression. 'I go out as little as I can,' one eighteen-year-old girl told me, 'and never to dances or clubs. I have this large bust and, everywhere I go, I know people are looking at me and wondering to themselves.'

This conviction is hard to break down; but in one instance it was done by sheer observation. A woman whose hands shook when she was anxious, and who was certain that she looked terrible and that people singled her out and noticed her, was one of a group of social phobics being taken on a bus by a therapist. The therapist kept running up and down the stairs, checking on his various patients; and the bus conductor turned to this woman and said, 'Look at that peculiar man: what on earth is he doing?' The woman laughed, and her fear of being noticed herself suddenly went. Other social phobics may need longer to build up their confidence; but it can be done.

5
School Phobia

'It was a long time before I could give it a name, and longer still before I let her give it a name. When I did, she was relieved; she did not want to go on making excuses.'

The name was 'school phobia'. And the mother was speaking about her fifteen-year-old daughter, who had suffered from it for several years. The phobia may have had its origin in several unpleasant experiences in hospital when she was a child, but it didn't become a problem until she passed her eleven-plus exam and went to a grammar school. 'Her father was away at the time, and it was a new and threatening situation for her,' said the mother. 'She began to have difficulties in getting there. During her first year, I found she was getting more and more psychosomatic illnesses and then she started coming home saying she had missed the bus. It became more and more difficult. Every day there was a different excuse or illness. Two or three mornings a week she would miss the bus. I then arranged for an older girl to walk with her, which worked for a while, but then she said there were too many people about. My husband tried taking her in the car, but there were too many arguments as she would always be late and making excuses. It was her fear of being outside the house. She was overwhelmed. It was nothing she could name; but she always felt that something would happen with which she could not cope.'

At the end of her first year, the head-mistress phoned the parents.

Apparently Pamela – whenever she did manage to get to school – was spending most of her time in the library, hiding away. It was a vicious circle: she wouldn't go to class and was then afraid the teacher would be cross – so was even more afraid of going to class. 'Teachers can be punitive,' said the mother. 'I have seen the blind panic on her face; and these panic attacks have so many repercussions, like vomiting and a lack of exercise through not going out, which leads to overweight.' She went to see the head-mistress, to put Pamela's case. At first there was a certain amount of scepticism, as the school had a lot of straightforward truancy; but since the mother has been liaising with the school, the attitude of both head-mistress and staff has softened. The mother also visited Pamela's various teachers, aware that one antagonistic teacher could put her back. The school, in fact, made every concession possible: Pamela could go any time she liked; and if she could not make the lesson, it was suggested she went to the library. She did not have to go into assembly – the ritual of this particularly frightened her – or wear school uniform. (She had put on weight and was very conscious of this in uniform. By wearing a smock instead she helped conceal her size.)

Pamela's attendance improved – although she could rarely manage more than three days of school a week. Then there were exams, and she was frightened off altogether for a fortnight. The mother arranged for her to see a psychiatrist – but this attempt failed, as she just didn't get up that day. She spent a great deal of her time in bed, in fact, feeling very depressed and inadequate. Her mother waited, then made another appointment some months later for her to see a psychotherapist (suggesting, this time, that it was to help Pamela's overweight problem). Fortunately, her daughter liked the psychotherapist. Since he has given her relaxation techniques, she has gained in confidence. It is the first adult contact she has made outside the family and shortly after her first few visits, she managed school for two weeks without a break. She has not kept this up, but her mother is hopeful.

'I have had to devote myself to her,' said the mother. 'My husband is working away from home now and, since this, the two of them have been getting along much better. Before, it was pretty unbearable, because they quarrelled. The child really became a tyrant in the family – not because of a desire for power, but through weakness.'

'School phobia' naturally tends to provoke adult cynicism and be regarded as a new name for skiving ('that's what it was called in my young days'). Only in recent years has school phobia been recognised and understood by an increasing number of schools. For example, Croydon's education department ran a scheme in which 50 children, with problems which included school phobia, were taught separately from the rest of the school. The children were broken up into small groups, each with their own teacher; and the understanding given to these 'withdrawal' groups helped them back to the main school.

School phobia at its mildest is almost universal: it is only severe in about one child in 700, usually at the age of around eleven or twelve. Some such children won't even get dressed for school; others will get dressed, but won't leave home; others will walk to school with their parents, but won't go in; yet others will go in to school with a parent, but refuse to stay when the parent leaves. Freud felt this 'separation' anxiety was the tension the child developed when without his mother; Anna Freud has attributed it to being a defence against the hostile fantasies the child has about his mother: by being with the mother, the child can see his fantasies have not come true.

There are a number of reasons for the onset of school phobia. Perhaps most frequently it is when the child changes from a small primary school where he feels safe, to a larger and more frightening one. In *The Gates*, a lively, autobiographical novel about school phobia, written by two boys from the East End of London, one of the characters recalls his feelings as he started at his new, massive comprehensive school, with 1,900 boys (to him, all seven feet tall): 'He could remember the first day clearly. He remembered walking towards the big black iron gates, and into the much bigger playground. He was nervous, but not terrified, at that stage. There seemed to be millions of uniforms everywhere, and so much noise. He had never heard anything like it in his life.'

Later, when explaining his constant running away to a psychiatrist, the boy says: 'I reach the gates and suddenly I just get so scared I have to run away. I just can't face the thought of school . . . I know nothing's going to happen to me, but every time I'm in school I just have to get out. I feel as if I'm trapped.' This feeling was echoed by the other main character in the book: 'Geoff had always feared being in a hall or classroom where everyone had to be quiet and he would sit in his chair and know that if he became dizzy he would not be able to get out without everyone looking at him, or the teacher calling him back and asking him in front of all the school why he wanted to go out.'

Sometimes, the phobia sets in after the child has been going to school for some time. This may be because he is having problems at school over his relationships with other children, so feels more secure at home. He may have some physical defect – such as being fat – which causes teasing at school, or he may have been away ill for some time. He may feel ashamed at not being good at games or work, or he may be having adolescent problems. Against such a background, any additional stress will cause outright school refusal. This could be a bullying act at school, a change of teacher, the illness or death of a relation, the breakdown of parents' marriage, an accident occurring to the child, or the birth of a sister or brother.

The child's fears take a physical form and he develops, say, sickness, diarrhoea and stomach pains at the time he should be leaving for school. In a study in 1960 of 50 school phobic children, L. A. Hersov found that the refusal to go to school developed gradually in 64 per cent of the cases – ending in point blank refusal. In 38 per cent of the cases it started after a change of school and in 18 per cent after the death, departure or illness of a parent. When the children were pressurised into going to school, the result was sweating, trembling and apparent faintness. A child may also complain of a cough or cold or ear trouble – anything that will persuade his parents to keep him away from school. As the parents realise that the refusal to go to school comes before the actual illness, they are naturally suspicious – particularly when the symptoms subside once the time for going to school has passed.

In some cases, the surface problems at school originate from relationships at home. Hersov found three patterns here: first, an over-indulgent mother and an inadequate, passive father. Second, a severe controlling mother and a passive father. Third, a firm controlling father and an over-indulgent mother. There is no evidence of a direct link with school phobia, but a child's over-close relationship with his mother can play a large part.

Deficiencies in the mother's own personality, as A. H. Denney points out in *Truancy and School Phobias*, can also be reflected in the child. If she is emotionally immature or unstable, then the child's stability will suffer. He quotes the case of a girl who started well at secondary school, but then developed aches and pains, became depressed about her work, and finally refused to attend school after seeing a dog run over by a car. She constantly expressed anxiety about her mother when away from her. Her mother, having experienced an unhappy childhood herself, had tended to over-mother her daughter in compensation. The child's recovery began when her mother became more mature, she regained her self-confidence and was later able to go back to school.

A child's home background was also stressed to me by Dr Leon Salzman, Clinical Professor of Psychiatry at the Albert Einstein College of Medicine, Bronx, New York: 'The youngest child, or one who has an overwhelming need for security, cannot manage on his own, particularly if he is over-indulged. A child who has grown up with his security wound up in his mother will fear being hurt by other kids and will get all kinds of phobias in contrast to the kid who has enough security to manage when his mother is absent. One woman I know, for instance, who has a three-year-old child, never lets it out of her sight for one minute. So even if she goes down the hall, the kid comes screaming out after her. Ultimately, this child will be severely damaged.

'When you go to school, it's a period of separation. For the first time, the child no longer has his guaranteed servant and has to share the teacher who doesn't see him as the only pebble on the beach. Many children cannot tolerate this, so refuse school. They are often very easily treated, as it's mostly just that the parent doesn't understand what the kid is up to. If they just visit the school two or three times, this will give the child security and help overcome school phobia.'

One school phobic told me that overprotectiveness on the part of her parents had made it difficult for her to face up to school, as they had always shielded her from anything unpleasant. 'From a very early age I dreaded going to school and would pretend to have stomach pains so that I would be kept at home. I actually did feel ill and for a long time I was sick every morning, and my mother used to keep me away from school. This situation did improve for a while until I had to go to my second school when I was eleven years old. This meant a bus journey of half an hour and I had never been on a bus on my own before. A month went by before I felt settled at my new school, but I was never really happy there.' At thirteen, she had to change to the main building of the school which was about a mile away. She really hated this place as it was a large, modern building in which she was always scared of getting lost.

'Shortly after this, I was sitting in class one morning and dying to spend a penny, but didn't like to go out in front of everyone. To my utter horror, I lost control and wet myself. I sat there panic-stricken until the lesson ended.' She was extremely upset about what had happened, but tried not to let it worry her. But during assembly one day she had her first really bad panic about not being able to get to the lavatory in time, and that night at home woke up shaking and crying. Her panics worsened; she tried to go back to school, but had to leave for good.

In certain cases of school phobia, where the child has become over-dependent on the mother, or the emotional climate at home is difficult, it can help to send him to a residential school. Most school phobics, however, are treated as outpatients. Sometimes cases are referred to the school medical officer from teachers, educational welfare officers or educational psychologists. The school medical officer then decides whether to recommend psychiatric treatment. After assessing the local services, he decides if the child would benefit more from, say, being referred to the child guidance clinic, or an assessment centre or hospital, or a special school.

Children may dislike being sent to a special school. As one character in *The Gates* said, 'I bet there's going to be a load of screaming mad kids there.' When he got there, he asked why it was meant to help. 'Most problem children just can't take the pressure of a normal school,' was the reply, 'whatever their problem is. You see, in a normal school they're being pressurised all the time. "Do this. Do that," and if children have problems at home, then they just can't cope with anything in school. They start playing truant and they disrupt the class . . . here, he's not pressurised and also he's seeing the psychiatrist and having treatment and that helps him overcome his problem.' It is important that these reasons are explained to a school phobic, who otherwise might feel he has been written off.

One drastic, though successful, treatment of a school phobic was given in a paper called *Treatment of a school phobia with implosive therapy*. In this case, an American boy called Billy, aged thirteen, had been absent from school for seven weeks. His phobic symptoms developed after a three-week absence from school due to illness. On the day he returned, Billy became extremely anxious, couldn't eat breakfast, and complained of severe chest pains. On arriving at school, he began to tremble, perspire profusely and cry. His chest pains became so severe that the headmaster insisted he see a doctor. The symptoms gradually disappeared, only to reappear the next morning. Neither force nor cajolery could get him to school, and his parents took him for treatment at a psychological centre.

At the time the child's phobia began, he had recently moved to a large new junior school and, due to increased competition in the new school and ill-health, his school work had deteriorated. (For these same health reasons, his mother was over-protective.) However, at his assessment interview, he was unable to explain his aversion to school.

Billy was asked to minutely describe a typical school day. It seemed mathematics and literature classes made him particularly anxious; so did the idea of being called on in class, being unable to answer the question and being laughed at. He was seen for six daily sessions. At each one, he was told a story, based on his own ad-

mitted fears, but highly exaggerated and horrific. A selection of the
scenes below was used in each story session and the therapist
repeated them until the child's anxiety – at first high – was visibly
reduced.

1 Billy is woken up and ordered to dress and come to breakfast.
   During breakfast his parents neither speak nor look at him.
2 Billy is ordered into the car by a cold and rejecting mother. It is
   emphasised how 'different' she seems. The suspense increases as
   the car moves towards town and he wonders and fears what will
   happen to him. Presently, he sees the school looming up.
3 Step by step Billy slowly approaches the school, being half
   dragged by his grim and silent mother. His eyes are glued to the
   building and many evil, laughing faces appear in the windows and
   then disappear.
4 After walking through the halls of the school, which are deserted
   and strangely silent, Billy finds himself at the stage door of the
   auditorium. The door opens and Billy is confronted by the school
   principal, who leers and says sadistically, 'We have all been
   waiting for you.' He can hear voices from inside chanting, 'We
   want Billy.' He looks to his mother for assistance but she says
   coldly, 'I'm through taking care of you. You're on your own
   from now.' And leaves.
5 Billy is half-dragged by the principal onto the stage. The place is
   filled with students and teachers, all of whom are laughing and
   jeering at him. The parents of all the pupils, including his own,·
   file in. Billy's parents are described as behaving in a cold, rejecting
   way.
6 While on stage, Billy, with spotlights in his face, is examined by
   each of his teachers, who ask him questions which he cannot begin
   to answer. He is being examined 'to find out what he has learned
   on vacation'. The gym teacher removes Billy's shirt and demands
   30 pushups, which he is unable to complete. The audience jeers,
   chants, and stares at him with hate-filled, menacing eyes.
7 Billy is ordered to his literature classroom by the principal. The
   room is dark and strange, and the chairs have been pushed to the

sides of the room. Students begin silently filing into the room. It is too dark to identify them. Tension grows as Billy wonders what will happen. The students encircle him, pressing ever closer, and begin to murmur, 'Crazy Billy' and 'stupid, stupid, stupid'. They then begin to jostle and strike him.

8 Billy enters the deserted library where he expects to take more tests. Fellow students enter the room and jeer while each teacher asks impossible questions in a rapid-fire manner.

9 He boards his school bus for the first time since his absence began. The bus driver is described as thick-skinned, ape-like, sinister and evil looking. [At this point Billy, through tears, sobbed 'But that's what our driver looks like!']. The students on the bus stare silently and malignantly at the patient as the bus veers from its normal route and enters a forest. When the bus stops, the silent students slowly move toward the patient and jostle him.

At the end of the first session, Billy showed extreme anxiety and was in tears, but obeyed the order to go to his feared maths class at school, and the moderate anxiety he felt disappeared during class. He returned to the clinic in good spirits; and by the end of the sixth session his anxiety at school had ceased – and had not returned at a 13-week follow-up.

In a pilot study carried out in 1969 by Charles J. Rabiner and Donald F. Klein (*Imipramine treatment of school phobia*), 24 out of the 28 children given Imipramine returned to school successfully, 85 per cent with improved behaviour. (Imipramine was used as it had been found successful in quelling panic attacks in adult agoraphobics.) The conclusion was that Imipramine prevented panic attacks stemming from separation anxiety.

'School phobia' is also present in college students, except that it can usually be narrowed down more exactly to 'examination phobia' – well known to college and university doctors. A fear of failure, and of disappointing one's parents, is usually behind it. The result is that the student walks out of the exam or develops physical symptoms which prevent him from taking it.

Dr Robert Sharpe, who helps run the student health service at London University, holds examination seminars to teach exam phobics 'anxiety management'. 'The first thing I want to know,' he said, 'is what the circumstances are surrounding the phobia. A very severe fear of criticism? Parental pressure? Exam phobics get physically screwed up, tense and perspiring. They also feel they don't want to take the exam: they rationalise and say they don't need it.

'I see each phobic personally first, for three or four hours of behavioural analysis. Then I have three sessions, of about three hours each, when I teach a group of them points about exam techniques, and give them a comprehensive personal view of how to treat the exam system. Some don't know how to deal with exams or examiners. There are ways of getting more marks by presenting work craftily; so we spend three hours going through methods of presentation in great detail. I tell them how to attract the examiner's eye with a good opening sentence; to let their rough work be seen, so that the examiner can follow the way their mind is working if they have insufficient time to finish; not to panic when all ten questions are incomprehensible but to direct any related knowledge towards the question.

'I also tell them to deduct 15 minutes from their overall time to choose the best questions; another 10 at the end to look through their paper and correct spelling mistakes; and a further 10 minutes for planning. The best order for answering exam papers is to take your pet subject first, then the easy question and finally one on which you have to grub around a bit. I forbid people to walk out of an exam before the end. I give mock exam papers and look for economy of expression; and at the end of the time allowed for each question, I cut in and tell them to start the next. There is no replacement for *in vivo* training, and learning under stress conditions. I create the exam anxiety, then fade it out.'

Examination phobia is rather less emotionally complex than school phobia. However, 'work phobia' is really more closely allied to school phobia than to examination phobia – as work phobia often arises through anxiety at separation from an over-protective wife, and school phobia is associated particularly with separation from an over-protective mother. So examination phobia can be treated on an individual basis. But school phobia and work phobia usually both involve casework with the whole family before they can be successfully overcome.

6

Thunderstorm Phobia

'It is not just that I am afraid: it goes much deeper than that. Hours before a thunderstorm, or if one is within 50 or 60 miles of me, I know about it and cannot sleep, eat or sometimes even move, even if we don't actually have a storm. Over the years it has been more or less a joke in the family, so rather than be a nuisance to others, I live alone. I am tied to my weather reports, even ringing for the local one, and I may say I am more often right than they are. I have partly solved the trouble myself by living in a bungalow with a large cupboard in my hall, which has room for a chair, cushions, a shelf for a large torch, and an extra pair of spectacles. I shut all the doors, pull a thick curtain over the front one, which is partly glass, and try to read. My doctor tells me he cannot help, a storm being so unpredictable that if I had pills to put me out, it may not come.'

Many of these points were reaffirmed by thunderstorm phobics who took part in an unpublished survey carried out by a psychologist, Austin Sinnott, at the University of Liverpool in 1975. (The vast majority of these were women, with an average age of fifty.) What was particularly noticeable was not so much the actual fear response on the day of the storm, but the obsessive preoccupation with the weather beforehand. Many also reported physiological effects from an oncoming storm, such as pressure over forehead and eyes. ('They all thought of themselves as barometers,' said Austin Sinnott.) Once the storm came, they invariably took avoidance action – going into cupboards under the stairs; burying their heads in pillows.

Two methods of treatment were tried out: first, discussion groups; second, treatment by desensitisation – that is, relaxing a group of patients and then, in a darkened room, playing amplified tape-recordings of thunderstorms, together with simulated lightning and an imaginary account of the violence of the storm. 'In the discussion group, we talked about the symptoms,' said Austin Sinnott, 'and also factual things about thunder and lightning: the possibility of being struck and the best place to go. A realistic attitude was encouraged.' Although the phobics were obviously helped by finding that others had the same intense fear about storms, progress was only gradual and quite a few dropped out of the group before the end of the sessions. ('I think I'm getting worse listening to people talking about it,' said one woman.)

The desensitisation groups had quite good results, however, with a lot of the phobics reporting that they were no longer bothered by storms after the treatment.

Storms can't be conjured up to order, so tape-recordings have to be used. But because they are just recordings, they are naturally not always successful. One woman told me that, 'The psychiatrist at a London teaching hospital said the only thing he could do was to put me in a very dark room, put on some tape records of storms borrowed from the B.B.C., and have some sort of instrument monitoring me. When the fear was at its peak, he would give me an injection and cool me down. But knowing he would be in the next room and it was just a tape-recording, I knew nothing would happen.'

The Liverpool survey found that about a third of the phobics had become so in childhood, due to the fear exhibited by one or other of their parents. Another third, whose phobia had come later in life, attributed it to a specific, really bad storm. And the final third, who had a high anxiety level, were subject to various phobias – though thunder was the main one.

Many parents – especially mothers – worry about passing on their fears to their children, but this particularly seems to happen in the case of storms. The noise is frightening to a child anyway, and to see an adult literally running into a cupboard only cements the fear. One phobic said: 'My fears must be inherited, as my grandfather would cover cutlery and mirrors when a storm was coming on; and my mother would take me into a dark cupboard. I would cover my eyes with a cushion so as not to see the lightning.' Another phobic's father would unplug the aerial and disconnect all the plugs if a storm came, which impressed him with a sense of danger, as his father was a very calm character.

It is not only children who 'catch' fear. One woman told me that she took her dog, previously quite unafraid of storms, with her when she went to stay at a friend's house. While there, there was a bad storm and her friend's dog rushed around, yelping with fear. The next time there was a storm, the woman found that her *own* dog promptly started to yelp.

The basic fear is of either the noise of the thunder, or of being hit by lightning. One man said: 'It doesn't matter how many people I am with, I am still certain my number is on the next flash. Lightning, statistically, kills. I used to carry the odds against being struck by lightning to try and reassure myself.' There are some, however, who cannot explain their fears: 'I only have to hear the weather man mention a storm,' said one phobic, 'and I am filled with fore-boding and dread. It's like doom hanging over me, as I wait for one to break.' Another agreed: 'I get a feeling of dread when the sky clouds over and becomes black. I think I am afraid of it becoming completely black during the day and then – perhaps? – the world ending. My only suggestion for the cause is that when I was small I was told of an avenging God in the sky, and maybe this memory has remained in my subconscious.'

Whatever the reason, this particular phobia can disrupt a person's life. Not only is there the obsessive concern with reading and listening to weather forecasts, but phobics won't leave the house either during a storm or if one is threatened. One woman, a Hungarian, said that it had decided the very country she lived in. When she and her husband left Hungary during the revolution, they had a choice of several countries to re-settle in. She chose England, because she was told it had comparatively few storms.

But her luck hasn't held: in one year recently, there were more storms in her area than in the previous sixteen years.

'At the end of March each year,' she said, 'I start getting agitated because summer is coming and that means thunderstorms. I have been afraid since my early twenties, but the last three years have been the worst. I have such a heartbeat that for hours after a storm my whole left side is painful. Every time I promise myself that was the last time, I would rather kill myself than it happen again. I say I will stay in the room, but when it comes I am a jelly, reduced to nothing. I have a little cupboard and I go there. I press my eyes so hard I can't see for about an hour; and if I sit in the cupboard over an hour, my husband has to straighten me up.

'I went to Hungary last summer and there were storms every second day, which normally never happens. I couldn't sleep and was afraid I would suffocate myself as I had to put a pillow over my head, plus a blanket. I was completely wet and unable to breathe. I had bright shiny spots in front of my eyes and my ears physically hurt. The whole time I was sweaty, shaking, dry-mouthed and headachy. I had three different kinds of tranquillisers, but they didn't do anything. I would die if somebody put me out in the garden during a storm, although last year I was caught in one coming home. My husband said, how did you do it? I know I came in next to the fences, like a blind person, with my eyes closed.'

Recently, she made an appointment to see a psychiatrist, feeling the fee was worth it. He tried to get to the origin of her fear, and finally put it down to it being an aftermath of the war, because she had spent so much time in a dark cellar in her home, during the invasion by Germany and then Russia, just listening to continuous bombing. Although she went for treatment some half a dozen times, nothing really happened, and she finally stopped going.

'My employers have been very understanding,' she said. 'I go to the toilet if there's a storm, to cover up my eyes – which is so stupid, as if the lightning hits me, it will be a very undignified death. What particularly worries me is that, as I am the supervisor at work, my staff can't look up to me or respect me.'

It is important to break this habit of avoidance if any improvement is to take place, and this can be done by finding out just how a phobic reacts in a storm and trying to change the pattern. The patient of one psychologist, for example, works at a desk in a glassed-off alcove. During a thunderstorm, she will make any excuse not to be at her desk, and he has asked specifically that she sit there. She had also always insisted that her husband brought her along for treatment, in case of a storm, and the husband was told to refuse to do this – and since then she has managed to go alone. 'Every thunderstorm phobic has some place to go and hide,' said her psychologist, 'and this place should be avoided. If possible, they should carry on with what they are doing; but if this is not possible, they should have some fixed, simple task to do. When a thunderstorm comes, I suggest they make endless cups of tea; get on with the book they are reading; clean out a cupboard and so on.'

Many of the phobics I came across had shopped around for treatment rather hopelessly. One woman, whose phobia had set in shortly after marriage and had lasted eighteen years, said that she had consulted her doctor and, over a period of some years, had taken tranquillisers by the hundred. She then visited a psychiatrist who promptly told her she was wasting his time, and she should go out and get a job. 'In desperation,' she said, 'I answered an advertisement by a hypnotist who at last understood my problem and set about putting me at my ease. He taught me how to relax – something I had long forgotten how to do. After a period of eight treatments, I was a changed person.'

It is hard, however, to go on looking for treatment after you have been rebuffed. One husband, in talking about his wife's storm phobia, said: 'Our own doctor just couldn't care less and tells my wife not to be so silly.' His wife has now reached the stage when she becomes nearly hysterical when a weather forecaster announces the possibility of thundery showers and, in an actual storm or when clouds begin to gather, she is uncontrollable. Her fear has now extended to heavy rain and strong winds and is getting worse.

The fear of the wind alone is also shared by many other people. 'Just the start of a breeze makes me quite ill,' said one. 'I'm almost out of my mind when it's windy.' And the mother of one girl said that her daughter, too, worried about a light breeze: 'She stands at the window watching the trees, waiting for it to get worse. As she has two small children, this upsets them because she sits and cries. She is always waiting for the weather forecast to come on the television and if they mention wind, she never eats all day. We have tried everything, but her husband and I have run out of words now.'

Related to thunderstorm phobia is a more general fear of noise. One woman was affected by practically any noise: 'Some make me so hysterical that I feel quite desperate: small droning noises such as from an electric fire or radio or television, if they are continuous and above a certain level of sound; ticking clocks; car engines; machinery. Pneumatic drills and generators pretty well drive me to madness.'

A certain level of noise – whether made by juggernauts or supersonic aircraft – is accepted nowadays by most people as part of the stress of urban life. Very few become phobic about minor bangs. However, the crash of a thunderstorm creates a more primitive fear – producing, in phobics, an overwhelming need to take cover. The extent of this automatic avoidance of a storm was well illustrated by one phobic – ironically, during treatment to cure this reaction. The therapist was trying to create the effect of a storm by tape-recordings of thunder. While he was energetically turning the light on and off to simulate lightning, he noticed that the patient's anxiety level had suddenly dropped. As it stayed down, he asked her what she was thinking about – and, after further probing, he discovered that she had (mentally) found a ditch and was hiding in it from his false storm.

7

Animal Phobias

Cats, Dogs, Horses, Chickens, Feathers,
Birds, Snakes

CATS

'If a cat rubbed against my legs, I would faint. I often dream that my bedroom is full of cats, even climbing up the walls or through the letter box.'

Cat lovers find it hard to understand the fear these animals can arouse in certain people. Yet cats are still associated by many with the supernatural and the uncanny. In almost all countries, it is thought that they have mystical powers for good or evil. According to medieval superstition, the black cat was Satan's favourite form and hence the witch's 'familiar'. Witches themselves were also believed to take cat-shape. Cats were also said to be fond of ghosts and purr when they encountered them, as well as being able to fore-tell the weather (when they claw at cushions, wind is coming; when they wash over their ears, it will rain.) Miners won't pronounce the word 'cat' when working in the mine; and at one time, in Cornwall, if a cat was found in a mine, no one would work on that level until it was killed. And although having a cat on board is lucky at sea, sailors avoid saying the name. There is also a belief that cats suck the breath of sleeping people, and kill babies this way.

The disadvantage of a fear of cats – as with other animals and insects – is that you encounter them unexpectedly, at any place and time. Cat phobics usually take the precaution of checking that their friends have no cat around before they visit them, but they are bound to come across them occasionally in the street, or the garden, and they often get nervous of going out at all. This was the case with one middle-aged housewife, who finally decided to try behaviour therapy treatment at a London hospital. I went along to the second session she had, as watching such treatment gives you a far greater insight into how a phobic feels, and how the therapist operates, than merely reading clinical accounts.

The patient had previously been assessed and asked if she had any other phobias; how long she had been a cat phobic; whether she could remember any precipitating incident; if it was a family trait; how she coped with the phobia; which aspects of the animal were most upsetting; which situations were most upsetting; how well she had adapted. Before treatment began, she was asked to complete a fear and avoidance scale, from 1 to 8, on various aspects of a cat. She rated herself as follows (the previous week's rating is in brackets):

colour	4	(6)
nearness	2	(8)
furriness	2	(4)
movement	6	(8)
height it's at	5	(8)

Scale

1 I am no more upset by this than the average person.
2 It makes me a little upset to think of it.
3 I feel quite uneasy to think of it.
4 It makes me particularly uneasy to think of it.
5 It frightens me to think of it.
6 It frightens me very much to think of it.
7 I can hardly bear to think about it.
8 The thought of it is terrifying.

The patient was then asked how she felt that day and rated herself as 4 on an anxiety scale of 1–10 (1 being not anxious: 10 being the most anxious ever felt). She was then given tablets to make her relax. At times throughout the treatment blood samples were taken and heart and skin changes monitored.

Therapist: How are you this week?

Patient: I have more faith in you. I did not have any last week, I just waited for the worst.

Therapist: It's going to be a less dreadful experience. For the moment, try to relax. I'll help you. And do these relaxing exercises the way I told you in your home. Do they work?

Patient: Yes.

Therapist: Close your eyes, not very tight and listen to what I say. Try to relax, relax, don't think of anything, just focus your attention on your body muscles, try to focus your attention on your toes, relax your right toes, relax your left toes, feel your feet are relaxed, the ankles are relaxed, the right foot is relaxed, now the left foot is relaxed, now the right leg, now the left leg, feel the knees are relaxed, feel that both of the lower limbs are relaxed. Think of your eyes, feel the right eye is relaxed, now the left. You're very relaxed. Don't think of anything, just relax. You can relax, just try to relax. Relax the muscles of the back, try to focus your attention on your fingers, the left hand, the thumb is relaxed, the fingers are relaxed, the arms are relaxed, the upper arms are relaxed, now the shoulders, the shoulders are relaxed, you can feel the shoulders are drooping, sagging down. Think of the muscles of the forehead, the muscles of the cheek are relaxed, the muscles of the back of the neck are relaxed, the muscles of the jaw are relaxed, the chin, every muscle of the body is relaxed, very well relaxed. The body feels very heavy and relaxed and you couldn't lift any part of your body even if you tried. Relax your body. Don't think of anything, just listen to me, relax your forehead muscles, relax the muscle above the ears, the neck muscles, the shoulders, the arms, the wrists, the hands, the muscles of the back, every part of you is relaxed, it's a very soothing experience, just relax, completely relax, you are not thinking about anything, and you can go to sleep if you feel like it. Relax, a very nice experience, your whole body is relaxed, every muscle of your body is relaxed. You can't move your feet, you can't move your fingers, not thinking of anything, just trying to relax, it's a wonderful experience, very relaxed, how calm the mind is, how quiet, how soothing. Every part of the body is relaxed.

You really do feel relaxed?

Patient: Almost completely, as much as I can be.

Therapist: You did very well.

At this point a nurse, the owner of a cat she was holding in a box, brought it in and took it over to the far side of the room.

Therapist: You remember this cat from last week?

Patient: I remember everything about her: she had lost her left eye.

Therapist: You don't have to worry, it's a very nice cat. We will keep it distant from you for the moment. You don't believe us, do you, when we say there will not be any surprise. We did not give you a surprise last week, did we?

Patient: No. The surprise was seeing the cat immediately.

Therapist: Well, we are telling you that it is here. The nurse is here. Try to relax.

Patient: I feel better this week.

Therapist: I am sure this cat must be the most friendly cat because it has helped you to get out of this fear. Did you not feel better last week? Did you see any cats? Was it less frightening than before?

Patient: The very next day after treatment, a cat was on the wall in the garden and I faced it and I shushed it away myself; my family couldn't believe it. I couldn't look at them before, even the face.

Therapist: We're going to put the cat in the box right here. I have
promised I would keep it at a distance. You don't have
to do anything with the cat, you just have to look at it,
the same exercise as last week. We will not do anything
you feel you cannot do. Once you get the confidence and
feel you can look at the cat, we can bring it nearer.

Patient: I am much better this week, so I will see. I did touch it
last week.

Therapist: You did very well last week. Let's bring it a bit nearer.
(Patient sits further back in her chair and watches it
nervously.) You don't have to worry, the nurse is just
stroking it. Just look at the cat, that's all. She's behaving
very well today. Perhaps it would like to play with me.
(Cat paws his hand.) She really doesn't hurt me at all.
You remember you touched her last week? Would
you like to be friendly to her again? (Cat then tries
to leap out of box: patient sits, hands clenched,
watching it.)

You are doing very well. It obviously doesn't make any
difference to you whether the cat is sitting there or not.
See how friendly the cat is trying to become. Just keep on
looking at its face. It's remarkable how well you are
doing today.

Patient: You've convinced me that she's got a very nice face.

Therapist: Would you like her a bit closer to you?

Patient: I don't mind.

Therapist: Does this change of distance make any difference?

Patient: No, not so much.

Therapist: Does it make a difference that she's in a box and not on
a lap?

Patient: As long as she's not on the floor.

Therapist: Can you look at her face? It's not as repulsive as you
had thought?

Patient: Not really.

Therapist: Can you look at all parts of her body without anxiety?

Patient: I am still not happy about her eyes.

Therapist: You think the cat would get down and jump at you?

Patient: Yes.

Therapist: But if it did jump at you, what would you do?

Patient: I don't know.

Therapist: Start putting your hand on it.

Patient: No.

Therapist: Let's bring it a bit nearer to you. I am sure you are feeling very comfortable in the presence of this cat. It's got beautiful ears (both therapist and nurse stroke the cat). Do you feel as anxious about this cat at this distance as when it was 5 ft away?

Patient: I am just as comfortable. The thing is, if I was not tied up to this apparatus, I would be happier. I can't avoid it if it jumps out at me.

Therapist: Think of the worst thing that can happen if it jumps out: it will touch your body, it will scratch your body. What else?

Patient: I don't know: that's all it can do.

Therapist: If some cat jumped at me, I would be frightened, but it wouldn't make me unable to look at the cat. Do you wish to touch it?

Patient: I don't mind.

Therapist: I'll bring it a bit closer to you.

Patient: Not too near.

Therapist: No, when you feel anxious, I will not bring it any further. I want you to be as comfortable as you are now, but still looking at the cat. (Cat's tail thrashes.) When you think you are feeling comfortable, tell me and I will bring it nearer. We won't do anything that you can't tolerate. (Patient tries to stroke cat, which turns around.) All right. If you don't show anxiety, then it will be all right. (Patient strokes it.) That's wonderful. (Cat moves; patient takes hand away.) First control your anxiety. (Patient now a bit tearful.) Does it make you very anxious, touching the cat?

Patient: Yes. I don't know what I am frightened of.

(Cat lashes out and patient jumps. Nurse shows patient that cat has not scratched her, despite this.)

Patient: It was because you were loving the cat so much last
(to nurse) week, I got to thinking perhaps there was something wrong with me.

Therapist: Would you be more comfortable if you touched it? (Patient's hand moves out slowly, nervously, but she does.) That's wonderful, that's remarkable. What do you think about it? You are doing very well. I am sure you never expected to do this. See how quiet it is, how calm. Try to be relaxed, if you are anxious and frightened, it will sense it. (He takes her hand.) It's lovely, isn't it. How do you feel?

Patient: Not very good.

(Cat then bites therapist, patient jumps, so, for that matter, does therapist.)

Therapist: (Showing her the hand the cat bit) It did not hurt me. When you were stroking it last, were you aware of any uncomfortable feelings, like increased heart beats?

Patient: No. (Jumps again as cat moves.)

Therapist: How do you feel?

Patient: It's just a bit near.

Therapist: Does it frighten you now?

Patient: A bit. I am not so nervous sitting next to it. The fur doesn't matter to me so much, because I feel its softness is nice. It's almost the least thing I worry about. (Cat lashes out.)

Therapist: (Soothingly) Even then she didn't bite you. If you met a cat on the roadside what would you do?

Patient: Cross on the other side of the road and run away, normally. This week I walked alongside. Last time helped such a lot.

Therapist: Do you think after this second treatment you are feeling a bit more confident?

Patient: Yes. I don't think I could ever hold it, but that doesn't matter. Looking at it is the thing: it was the look I couldn't take.

Therapist: I would like you to have the box in your lap. Nurse will help.

Patient: OK. (Gets very upset at first, then becomes better and strokes the cat, but still very unrelaxed.)

Therapist: Isn't that good. (Pats her on shoulder.)

Patient: She happens to be quite a nice cat. I am all right with her here, but when she's above me, I can't bear it. (The cat then lashes out and is taken off patient's lap.) I am getting a bit agitated, is there much longer to go? It's the sudden jump that frightens me, the slow movement doesn't.

Therapist: Does it make a difference if it moves?

Patient: It did last week, but not any more.

Therapist: Do you think you are completely cured?

Patient: When she jumps I get nervous, but a lot of people do.

Therapist: But it was not so frightening? You can relax now. Try and relax your body, there's no pressure on your body ... (this relaxation went on, as before, for five minutes or so).

The session lasted, in all, from 9.30 a.m. to 1 p.m. and, at the end, the patient rang her daughter to tell her, delightedly, how well it had gone. A follow-up was arranged for some weeks later, to check if the improvement was maintained and, before leaving, the patient rated herself as:

colour	2	(4 on arrival that day)
nearness	1	(2 on arrival)
furriness	0	(2 on arrival)
movement	3	(6 on arrival)
height cat at	4	(5 on arrival)

Although exposing a phobic directly to the feared object for pro-longed periods is usually a very successful treatment, some phobics prefer a gentler approach. In one case quoted in the *British Medical Journal* in 1960, a cat phobic – whose fear had extended to fur, too – handled, at her first session, a velvety material which was a bit like fur. She then went on to handle several materials which felt even more like fur, until she was able to stroke real fur without fear. The next move was to introduce her to pictures of cats and toy cats, and, at the end of a few weeks, she was able to hold a live kitten on her lap, and stroke it. She then looked after a kitten at the day hospital where she was taking treatment, took it home, and, after a few months, was then able to touch an adult cat. After ten weeks of treatment, cats no longer worried her.

The colour of a cat also affects a phobic. In *Some Approaches to the Treatment of Phobic Disorders*, R. Gaind, J. P. Watson and I. M. Marks describe the treatment of a cat phobic who had rated ginger cats as her worst enemy and black cats as her second worst. At 15-minute intervals, she had to look at a black cat and a ginger cat separately, six feet away, and for one minute each. In between times, she was exposed progressively to either the black cat or the ginger cat. Having to look at the cats initially sent her pulse up to almost 130; but when, after that, she was exposed to the black cat for 15 minutes, there was very little increase in heart rate. Her fear response to the ginger cat was less after her exposure to the black cat: during the second 15 minutes of exposure, the ginger cat was brought nearer and the patient touched it and then allowed it to touch her. As the session proceeded, every intensification of the situation brought on anxiety – which then subsided. An hour and a half after the start of treatment, the patient was cuddling the cats without anxiety.

Dr Alexandra Symonds, at New York University College of Medicine, told me that: 'If you ask phobics what it is about a cat that they don't like, they usually say, "they jump on the table; you never know what they are going to do". They are very often people who are afraid of spontaneity and you can't train animals to be completely predictable. It's the animal part of themselves, the joyful unpredictable part, that the phobics are trying to keep down.'

This dislike of a cat's jumpy habits was certainly mentioned to me by several cat phobics. One said her sister-in-law had recently bought a frisky black kitten: 'She never thought to let me know, so when she opened the door and I saw it, I nearly collapsed. My husband and I went in and I asked if they would put it in another room. They said it wouldn't touch me, and I sat there with my knuckles white. It is a horrible feeling, because cats definitely know when someone is afraid: they just sit and stare. This kitten did just that: my heart beat faster and I felt little jumps in my stomach and the sweat on my face. In the end, it dived and the shock just made me burst into tears.' Her neighbour has now bought a kitten, which spends most of its time on their shared back porch. As she daren't pass the kitten to go into the garden, she has to keep her small daughter inside to play.

DOGS

The fear of 'staring' was cited by another phobic in regard to dogs. Her worst fear is if they just stand and look at her, and she feels, too, that they not only sense, but actually enjoy, the paralysing fear that they can cause. She was unable to account for her fear, but another girl put it down to being bitten at the age of eight. She had already been rather unnerved by dogs several years earlier, when one of them had knocked her down. She started feeling afraid to pass dogs in the street and would cross the street, regardless of traffic, if she saw one. In her late teens, she had to stop delivering charity Christmas boxes rather than pass barking dogs. When, the following spring, she moved into a flat which had a dog next door, she spent half her time outside waiting for the dog to go into its house, and allow her to get into her room. Later on, she went to look for another room, but heard a dog barking when she knocked at the door and ran away. She discussed the problem with her father, who said that he had had a similar phobia, but that this had disappeared once he had analysed the reason for his fear. The girl, in turn, tried to analyse hers and decided that it was that dogs would rape her. She said this was partly because most people refer to dogs as 'he', so she thought of them as purely male. Also, whenever she tried to visualise what she feared, it was always being knocked over by a dog (as had happened previously). Since analysing her reason, she has not been so afraid.

Research carried out in 1966 by Marks and Gelder showed that most animal phobias occur, in fact, in women. These generally start before the age of eight. Until adolescence, they are common in both boys and girls, but after this time they usually persist only in girls, and are comparatively rare. In *Fears and Phobias*, Marks found that 3 per cent (24) of all phobics who came to Maudsley Hospital during the 1960s were animal phobics.

Marks also found that emotional problems can complicate matters. In a case quoted in *Fears and Phobias*, a married woman complained of dog phobia. This had started when she was eighteen months old, after being bitten and dragged out of the room by an Alsatian dog. She would avoid dogs without leads in the street by crossing the road, and would not go on walks in case she met a dog. She felt neglected by her husband and was having an affair with another man. Shortly after she began treatment, this other man left her. She became depressed, attempted suicide, and was finally referred to group psychotherapy. The dog phobia continued to affect her throughout these events.

Another case, reported in 1972 by Ben D. Monroe and C. Jonathan Ahr, describes the cure of dog phobia in a blind patient, by means of desensitisation. The patient was nineteen and at a pre-college entrance class for blind students. When she was five, she had been knocked down and roughed up by a large dog. Since then she had avoided them. Dogs running free brought more fear than dogs on a leash; she was more afraid when only one person was there than when several were; dogs touching her, or moving near her, frightened her more than a dog barking far away; and growling and barking dogs were more frightening than quiet dogs.

The patient was taken to a mental health centre, after a severe anxiety attack brought on by hearing dogs fighting outside her classroom. At the centre, she was interviewed and brief particulars taken; she was then helped to relax. This relaxation training then continued for another week or so, and she was encouraged to practise on her own. Meanwhile, a tape-recording of a barking dog was made, which increased in intensity and duration. At the beginning of each desensitisation session, the patient was relaxed and told to show any increase in anxiety by raising her right fore-finger. (When she did so, she was made to relax again, and the tape was reset at starting point.)

The tape started with the lowest volume setting and the shortest time of barking and was increased in duration only after it had been heard three times without provoking anxiety. Movement to a higher volume setting took place only when *all* durations of barking, at a given volume setting, had been successfully coped with by the patient. Desensitisation was completed in five sessions on consecu-tive days, by which time the patient had her fear under control. (Another phobic's attempt to cure herself did not end so success-fully: she summoned up the courage to buy a dog, left it in the house while she went out – and was then too afraid to go back inside.)

HORSES

Many individual cases of animal phobics have been reported by psychoanalysts. The most famous was that of 'Little Hans' in 1909. Hans was a four-year-old patient of Freud, and he suffered from a fear of horses. He was so convinced that a horse was going to bite him that he refused to go out into the street. His fear of horses, according to Freud's sex-oriented viewpoint, hid a more serious fear – namely, a fear of his father. And the reason why he was afraid of his father was his Oedipus complex; he had a sexual desire for his mother, which he thought would bring retribution (possibly castration) from his father. By forming a phobia, Freud concluded, Hans directed his castration anxiety to a different object: he was now no longer afraid of being castrated by his father, but of being bitten by a horse. And by refusing to leave the house in case he met a horse, he was able to end his anxiety. Freud himself, in fact, only saw Hans once: he interpreted the thoughts of this child through the conversations Hans's father had with the child – which were, in turn, communicated to Freud. Hans had to be told the things he could not say himself. (Like castration, perhaps?) The child's phobia finally went when he 'resolved' his Oedipus complex.

A more straightforward case of the way a phobia of horses developed was told to me by an adult woman who, at the age of four, went to her home town's annual carnival, which was always led by a man on horseback. Nervous of the horse, she ran out in the road; and can still remember looking up at two hooves, as the horse reared above her, before being pulled away by her mother, in time to avoid injury. The incident was reinforced when she was twelve, when a friend persuaded her to sit on a horse, which promptly bolted with her for half a mile or so. This made her hysterical and she did not recover for several days. In later years, when taking a course in graphic design, she was asked to illustrate a horse-box and horse equipment. This meant a trip to a farm to see some horses; and despite there being other students there, she was convinced the horses were singling her out and trying to bite her. She eventually burst into tears and had to leave. The fear is still as intense in adult life: being near a horse causes palpitations and sometimes physical sickness. The unexpected sight of a horse, in one instance, made her scream and run off – deserting a three-year-old child she was taking for a walk.

CHICKENS

Chickens may seem even more unlikely objects for a phobia than a horse, but unpleasant childhood experiences with them have resulted in phobias which had often spread to feathers and birds. One child of seven had jumped screaming on the table when her dog and cat started chasing a neighbour's chicken round the dining room, with feathers and fur flying. After that, she would never sleep on a pillow. She had another screaming fit when an elderly aunt bent down to kiss her while wearing a feathered hat, for fear of a feather coming out of it. The fear spread to birds, and still persists in adult life.

A woman, whose phobia is still mainly over chickens, though she is not happy within a yard or so of any bird, says it may have happened after she bumped into a Christmas turkey hanging up in the dark when she was a child. As, during the war, many people kept chickens, and would not think of mentioning it, she would often see them accidentally and go into hysterics. She tried several times to overcome her fears: 'Once, on a farm in Cornwall, the only toilets were in the farmyard surrounded by chickens. For the first few days, there was no chance of me going anywhere near that yard and I tramped over fields and hedges and went into villages to use the toilets. At night it was O.K., because they were all put away, but for one eccentric chicken that roosted every night on top of a hay-stack in the yard. Each night I shone my torch to make sure that horrible ginger body was up in the hay and nowhere near where I could trip over it.

'My husband made me stand as near to the yard full of chickens as I could bear, and asked me to stare at them closely and try and analyse what scared me so much; but, although I tried, I could not stare at them. But I did decide to venture the other side of the gate, with plenty of protectors on hand, and could then walk to the toilets with my eyes shut. Once I was in the safety of the toilet, it was O.K., except that I could see bobbing shadows going past under the door, and had to shout for help before I could open the door. By the end of a fortnight I could go out with just my sister to shoo them away and I was feeling a little braver. But one day when she clapped her hands, a chicken ran towards me instead of the other way. Once more, the horrible hysterics and back to square one.'

The same kind of occurrence proved the downfall of another phobic. In this case, her husband, a dairy farmer, had tried to cure her phobia by asking her to feed his chickens. But he forgot to tell her that, as soon as she started throwing the feed down, they would naturally all swoop towards her. They did so, and she screamed, dropped the grain, and refused to go near them again.

FEATHERS

Another sufferer, who is now nearly sixty, said that as long as she could remember she has had a horror of feathers: 'Just to look at them at close quarters makes me perspire; my hands go clammy and I feel as if my body was on fire. I think it started when I was about five and went with my mother to feed the chickens and I picked up one of the tiny chicks and, before I knew what had happened, I was on my back and a very angry hen was sitting on my face pecking at me. I still have some small scars on my face.' Some years ago, she was set on by a gander who pecked and hissed at her legs. No one was there to help, and she was so terrified that she caught hold of his long neck and swung him up high over her head into the next field. She then lost her voice for two weeks. She finally overcame her fear of feathers when she felt bound to rescue a small fledgling sparrow from some cats and was able to pick it up.

In a case recorded by D. F. Clark, in 1963, a thirty-one-year-old woman was treated for a phobia of birds and feathers. 'She was unable to go for walks out of doors, in parks or go to zoos with her two-year-old boy or to the seaside on holiday with her husband because of the possibility of having birds come near her or, worse still, swoop over her.' The treatment consisted of getting her to relax by suggestion and mild hypnosis. She was then shown a single feather, at a distance of 12 feet. The feather was moved nearer and nearer to her, unless she showed fear, in which case it was moved back again. After the patient was able to accept a single feather being held only a foot away, the next item – assorted feathers – was presented in the same way. This was followed by bags of feathers; then a bundle of feathers; then stuffed birds; and finally, live birds. The patient was also told, in between sessions at the hospital, to go to places where there were likely to be birds or feathers. She was told to remain calm, if possible, when she was near them, but to come away at once if she should feel afraid. At the end of the therapy, she 'could have handfuls of feathers flung at her, could plunge her hands into a bag of down and no longer feared going out of doors or birds in the garden and hedgerows'.

In another two cases of feather phobia reported by J. P. Watson and colleagues in 1971, treatment in imagination was used, at the patients' request, before real feathers, including a Red Indian head-dress, were presented. One of the phobics was a married woman of twenty-one, who asked for help in overcoming her long-standing feather phobia because she was getting increasingly worried that her children might bring home a feather. She couldn't bear to have feathered objects like pillows and certain toys in the house. The second case, of a thirty-year-old housewife, was referred by a psychotherapist, who hoped that if her phobia was cured it would help his treatment of her marital problems and depression. This phobic had recurrent nightmares about black feathers, couldn't stand feathered objects in her home and didn't like the country in case she came across a feather. Both phobics were greatly helped by the treatment.

Most feather phobics, however, are too embarrassed to admit to their phobia in case they are laughed at. One – who has had nightmares about feathers since she was three – once approached the psychology lecturer at her college, 'but he seemed amused and could shed no light'. 'Yet it's hard to disguise,' said another, 'as if someone happens to show me a feather or an actual bird, I literally go into hysterics. The other day I was walking along the sea front when, glancing up, I noticed a pigeon flapping its wings as though it was going to land on top of me. I ended up flat on the sea front screaming and crying.'

BIRDS

Bird phobics find themselves continually on the watch. 'When I'm in the house alone,' said one, 'I always keep the windows and outside doors closed, even in hot weather. We live in an old house which has fireplaces in every room. I had the bedroom ones taken out and the chimneys blocked up. Downstairs we have gas fires and I have had covers with small apertures made over these chimneys.' Unfortunately, her neighbour encourages birds, so she cannot go into the garden as the birds come quite close, especially the robins, and she is terrified. Another woman said she could not even put up with them on the window ledge outside the room she was in; and one phobic's holiday at Butlin's was spoilt because of the presence of a lot of tame sparrows there. 'I had to make a hasty exit from the ballroom twice when a sparrow flew in; and the last morning I had to run out and leave my breakfast because there was a bird hopping about on the tables.'

A pedestrian shopping centre has become a source of fear and embarrassment to one twenty-one-year-old girl as it is always infested with pigeons. She also watches cages in people's homes constantly in case the birds get out, and even dreams of them. It is always the same kind of dream: she walks into a building of some sort and suddenly the place is full of birds flying round her head: all she can do is scream. This girl believed her phobia began when she was four and her father bought her a budgerigar which got into her hair. Even now she still wants to cover her head when near birds.

This reaction, in fact, is fairly common among phobics – particularly with those whose first fear of birds came from being trapped in a room with a bird, or having a bird fly up at them suddenly. The sight or sound of fluttering wings is often one of the most feared factors: 'The only bird I can go anywhere near is a penguin and I presume this is because they haven't got big flapping wings.' 'I am not as bad when the birds are walking, it's when they spread their wings that I get this feeling of fear.' 'It's their horrible, knowing, fixed, beady eyes which look so evil and the shape of the small head out of proportion to the soft body and cruel looking claws, waiting a chance to attack. But when I get most terrified is when they are in the same room as me, fluttering to get out.'

This last phobic had more fear of dead birds than live ones ('all those stiff feathers and claws standing up in the air make me shudder'). Her phobia may have started, she thinks, when her older brothers used to get hold of the dead birds her father had shot, and flutter them at her. A fifty-eight-year-old woman, with the same phobia, thinks this may also have started when she was about four, when she was awakened by her father holding up a dead water-fowl which he had brought home. She is still afraid to walk through long grass in case she stands on one; and still feels the horror she felt when swimming in Italy and finding a great dead blackbird in the water beside her. The sight of birds struggling in oil is also particularly abhorrent to another phobic: 'The most disgusting image to me is a bedraggled bird, when its wings aren't folded away; and if it's black, like a crow, it's worse than if it's white, like a seagull. It's something about the look of them when they are collapsed. Nothing looks so destroyed.'

Although dead birds aren't so prevalent as live ones, they have a knack of turning up, according to the sufferers, in many a beauty spot and will ruin many a country – or even town – walk. One woman said that if she sees a dead bird lying in a street, she has to let go of any object she is holding as she imagines that the object is the bird. She doesn't mind so much if the bird has been squashed by a car; it's when it is in a perfect condition that she feels strange. She can't go into a museum where there are stuffed birds, and can't get a chicken ready if it hasn't been oven-prepared.

It was this innate fear of birds that Alfred Hitchcock successfully exploited in his film, *The Birds* (and which many phobics went masochistically along to see). 'They have a fascination,' said one. 'When I am in open spaces, the fear does not affect me so much and I can even see a certain beauty in the way they soar and in their singing. But I also see them in another way. They have evil fixed eyes which look at one sideways – and those terrible claws and legs.'

SNAKES

Snakes, too, are biblically linked with evil and are thought to be creatures of ill-omen. Indeed, in East Grinstead, Sussex, in 1936, the erection of a symbol depicting the serpent and staff of Aesculapius, the Greek God of Medicine, caused a public outcry. According to country tradition, a live adder on someone's doorstep was a warning of death to someone living there; and it is believed that adders cannot die before sunset, however badly injured they are. Another idea is that one could regain one's youth by feeding on snakes ('you have eat a snake and are grown young, gamesome and rampant' (*Elder Brother*, Beaumont and Fletcher)). On the credit side, the snake in mythology was often the symbol of healing and wisdom, and also of re-birth because it sloughs off its skin.

Freud considered the snake a phallic symbol, and Freudian interpretation of snake dreams or imagery is linked with sexual guilt or maladjustment – involving, for example, fears of intercourse or rape, inadequate sexual relationships and over preoccupation with sex. J. A. Hadfield, in *Dreams and Nightmares*, relates the following boy's dream:

'I dreamed of a snake [the male sex organ] which was exceedingly sensitive and delicate to the touch. It was restlessly moving to and fro. It was milky-white in colour. The snake does not seem to be attached to me in any way, nor am I holding it: it is just there, in mid-air! [The objectification and projection of his feelings.] Then fear came out of the end of this snake [the orgasm], and when it came the snake shrivelled up into nothing [end of the orgasm]. Then it turned into a vampire. I felt absolutely ripped open and went off into unconsciousness with this tension hanging over me ... there I was lying ripped open with this vampire over me. So I screamed out when the vampire came, and I cried out, "I won't do it again, I won't have anything to do with sex" [a reference to masturbation, which had brought it all on.]'

Hadfield's interpretation of this nightmare is that the snake is the penis, which is feared. The vampire came out of the penis, and represents the exhausting results of the orgasm. It also, according to the child, looked something like his mother – whose condemnation of sex had terrified him.

More practically, Ann Faraday in *The Dream Game* considers that the first question to ask yourself, after dreaming about a snake, is whether there are any snakes in your life at the present time. (Snakes as sex symbols in dreams are rare, in her experience.) The dream, she reasons, could be a warning about a snake you saw out of the corner of your eye in some bushes, but which did not register – as happened to her once. If there aren't any around – and it would be unlikely, on the whole, in Britain – then the dream snake symbolises someone or something in your life. You may *like* snakes – in which case the dream represents a force for good. But if you consider snakes as slimy and poisonous, then someone you are involved with (perhaps part of yourself) is like that.

This point was also made by Dr Alexandra Symonds of the New York University College of Medicine. She told me she had a patient 'who was very afraid of snakes and could not even look at a picture of a snake. When this patient talked to me about it, she said "snakes are cold-blooded" and then remembered an expression used in the south, "cold as a snake". This means a person who is mean and nasty and it represented a struggle within herself: it was an aspect of herself that she was trying to deny, as all these phobias have a symbolic meaning. The patient was terrified of her own hostility and mean, nasty feelings.'

Many believe that fears of snakes are innate. Monkeys, brought up in captivity without ever seeing a snake, still react with fear when first shown one. A fear of snakes is shown by most primates and is partly based on fear of their sudden, writhing movement. Human infants also show innate fear of intense, sudden or unexpected movement.

Latent childhood fears can often be worsened by actually seeing a snake, even in captivity. As Barry Lubetkin, Clinical Director at the Institute for Behavior Therapy, New York, pointed out: 'People have many misconceptions about snakes. They have been conditioned to avoid them, as they can be dangerous, they are slimy-looking and some are poisonous. Some have had a traumatising experience with a snake and then they would avoid the situation – and it becomes a full-blown phobia.' Sometimes there can be a delayed reaction. An English girl who had been collecting pieces of willow to make whistles, accidentally picked up a twig which was, in fact, a coat of an adder which had just been shed. She felt no fear; but six years later when she visited the reptile house at London Zoo, she got a phobic reaction, which she felt had its roots in the original episode.

No one I came across had been threatened or bitten by a snake. But as one girl said: 'It's not that I think the snake is going to kill me, the fact that it could be poisonous doesn't worry me: it's seeing the movement, feeling it's going to wrap itself round me, the evilness of it touching me. Even if I see a picture of one in a magazine, I get a strange sensation at the back of my neck and feel terribly vulnerable. The mental picture of one lying coiled up can be just as frightening. If I'm lying in bed, feeling low, I will go off at a tangent and start thinking about snakes; and although I know there isn't one at the bottom of the bed, I don't want to move my feet. If something unexpectedly touches my face, I jump – thinking it's a snake, although I know it isn't. I can work myself up into a terrible state thinking about them and have to try and be terribly strong-minded if I find myself doing it. But it is almost as if it's such a weakness that it strikes me when I am low.'

The idea of any treatment involving the sight of a snake seems to upset snake phobics more than most. One said she had never tried any treatment because she didn't know what actually happened and she was afraid of being shown a picture of a snake. 'If anyone brought me a snake in their hands, I would never set foot in that particular room again without keeping my eyes peeled all round; and I would never trust that person again.'

However, if a snake phobic can be persuaded to have treatment, it's been shown that 'tricking' them into thinking they have improved has in fact helped them to improve. S. Valins and A. A. Ray gave false heart rate recordings to snake phobics, giving them the impression that they were more relaxed, or less responsive, in the presence of snakes than they had thought; and this led to a reduction in their avoidance of a snake. (A control group, who heard the same sound of heartbeats, but were told this was irrelevant background noise, did not improve.) This implies that if a patient *thinks* he is relaxed in the presence of a feared object, he will 're-label' it 'non-threatening'.

In 1968, B. Ritter divided 44 children with fears of snakes into three different groups. The first group saw others take part in gradually increasing play with a tame snake. The second group not only saw others take part, but were gradually brought into physical contact with the snake itself. The last group had no treatment at all. Both the first two groups improved much more than the untreated group – the second group having the best results.

Donald Meichenbaum has carried out several studies into the effectiveness of getting phobics to talk to themselves during treatment, giving themselves instructions on how to cope. For example, in one study, when the patient heard the therapist say the word 'snake', he or she had to relate the thoughts and descriptive images she experienced when confronted with a snake (such as, 'it's ugly; it's slimy; I can't look at it'). After having made all these statements, the patient was then given an electric shock on the finger – to 'punish' these thoughts. The shock was ended when the patient gave herself a set of self-instructions, such as, 'Relax; I can touch it; one step at a time.' Patients were encouraged, over several sessions, to give themselves these instructions so that they could look at, touch and handle a snake, and were in control of how they felt. This, results showed, definitely helped reduce the patients' fears.

How do snake phobics actually feel when facing the situation they fear? Dr Manuel Zane, who started a phobia clinic in White Plains Hospital, New York, in 1971, had as a patient a twenty-four-year-old psychologist, who had suffered from an abnormal fear of snakes for ten years. She avoided libraries and bookstores in case she came across a picture of a snake; and in her work, she would not use testing materials that included the figure of a snake. As part of her treatment, Dr Zane helped her look at coloured pictures of snakes. Her first reaction was one of avoidance; then, as she touched one of the pictures, she claimed she could 'sense a roundness' and could feel the shape of the snake.

This illusion, part of the phobic reaction, was felt again when she looked at a picture of a coiled snake. ('It's colourful and it's fat; and this one is moving. It's wriggling along.' 'Which way?' asked Dr Zane. 'At me!' she said.) However, by laughing and talking to him, she reduced her stress and did not run away – which she would normally have done. She made the effort to look at the pictures again, reassuring herself and being reassured, that that was all they were. By concentration, she stopped 'the movement', and learnt that by staying in the situation she feared, rather than leaving it, she could control her reaction. Previously, the slightest allusion to a snake brought up an immediate rush of stored memories and she fled. 'I never knew it would fade,' she said, 'because when I'd get just a flash of a snake, it did everything it possibly could in an instant: it moved, I felt it. I saw it. I touched it. I heard it. Everything. You know, I'd never look at it long enough.'

This shows that the panic reactions to such things as snakes — and, indeed, animals too – are an automatic response of jumbled and fearful sensations which, when the patient talks about them and thinks them out, can often be lessened in intensity. Once such a phobic is able, for the first time, to confront the situation, and sort out overwhelming memories and sensations, she is immediately in a much better position to control her reactions.

8

Claustrophobia or the Fear of Confined Spaces

In *Rogue Male* by Geoffrey Household, the main character carves out a burrow for himself under the earth, where he can hide. Its size is eight feet long, four feet high, and three feet wide. On one occasion he only dares move out of it for a few hours over 13 days, because he is being hunted down. Then his enemies find him and, after hearing a thud, he realises they have trapped him in there by means of a tree trunk. 'I don't know what happened to me then ... my ears were drumming and my skin oozing cold sweat. I suppose that if you sit on hysteria long enough and hard enough, you lose consciousness. Something has to give way, and if the mind won't, the body must.' His attempts at digging himself out, in the next day or so, failed. 'It seemed to me at the time that I kept a remarkable control over myself. I concentrated on breathing in and out by the ventilator, forcing my mind to remain blank.'

Reading about people who are trapped – whether in potholes, mines or submarines – taps a nerve in most people. Indeed, probably more people suffer from varying degrees of claustrophobia than from any other phobia: so much so that the word has rather lost its force. Most of us will admit to a slight feeling of claustrophobia in crowded undergrounds or lifts – meaning, in effect, that we dislike being hemmed in or feeling trapped. Some, however, react with panic or severe stress in those situations: others cannot bear even to contemplate being in them. One man in his twenties, for example, has recently moved offices into one which is 16 floors up. Rather than go up by lift, he walks up and down the stairs – lunchtime included. It takes him five minutes to regain his breath on arrival, but he would resign rather than take the lift.

An idea of what goes through lift phobics' minds comes through in the following few excerpts from a group meeting of them, led by Dr Manuel Zane, who runs the phobia clinic in White Plains Hospital, New York.

Mrs S.:   I'm scared of any place where I'm hemmed in . . . subways, phone booths. Any place I'm locked up in and can't get out. I want out . . . right then . . . not later . . . right then.

Dr Zane: What's happening then? What are you feeling?

Mrs S.:   Afraid. Nothing particularly in my body. When the elevator gets to the floor, it goes slow. Sometimes it seems like it'll never get there. I'm more afraid if there are a lot of people in the elevator because I'm surrounded by people as well as being in that elevator. I wouldn't like to be there by myself. It scares the living daylights out of me. I think it's not going to make it. Has it stopped? I'm just watching the doors to see if they'll open.

Mrs T.:   I'm the same. I can't wait to get out. If the indicator lights are moving, I feel better because when it's going I know there's a chance of my getting out. But if those lights don't work or if there's no window in the elevator, I'm exceedingly uncomfortable . . . I get out of breath, very white and get into a cold sweat . . . I always try to get near the door, near the controls, especially in the more modern elevators where you can open the door and get more air. It seems to me the lack of air . . .

Mr O.:   That's it . . . suffocation.

Dr Zane: So basically it's being closed in. What about the thought of its getting stuck. Does that seem like a problem?

Mr O.:   I'm not afraid of it falling.

Mrs C.: I do have a fear that the elevator is going to break down. I feel I'm not going to be able to get out of it. As a matter of fact, when I get in I look at the ceiling to see how large the hole is ... to see if I can manage to get through it.[1]

Dr Zane has found group sessions like this to be effective, not only because they reach more people, but because they help the group to shape up solid ideas of what a phobia is all about; and lets them see that other people go through the same thing. Group sessions were part of his ten-week course for lift phobics, held for the first time in 1971. Meetings took place weekly, and each phobic had a voluntary, individual, therapist. The actual mechanism of lifts was explained to the phobics; and they were taught to avoid fear by looking at the lights, counting to themselves, or even talking to themselves. Finally, two therapists and two patients would go into a lift together. Afterwards everyone would meet and discuss their experiences. Once a week, the patient and his own therapist would also meet and try out the situation again. Gradually, although the patients were not without fear at first, they were able to cope.

In his office, Dr Zane also has a small, closed-in area, which can be locked – with the patient's consent. He first makes sure they can handle the situation with the door closed, but unlocked, and with the light on; and then progresses to turning out the light and locking the door. He monitors the person's reactions to each step in his attempt to find the connection between these automatic reactions and the person's thinking. His main object is to get the phobic less frightened about his own disturbing bodily reactions to the situation he fears. Zane would rather the patient come out when he feels upset, so that he can find out what is upsetting him. One four-year-old boy (whose parents had had to give up their 20th floor flat for one near the ground floor, due to his fear of lifts) had started his treatment in Dr Zane's lift. It was suggested he tried to let the lift door close, but he had put his hand out and stopped it 15 times before he could go to the next floor. Then, very excited by his

[1] This quoted extract © Manuel Zane 1975.

progress, he went home where he was encouraged to do the same
thing. After four or five attempts, he managed to go up in the lift.
Dr Zane thinks the ability to react with fear remains and, under
certain circumstances, may start up again. This is why he tried to
learn as much as possible about where that reaction originates.

One imaginative treatment of the fear of lifts was carried out by
Leslie Solyom and S. Bryntwick. Two male phobics were involved,
and both had previously received aversion relief therapy for their
fear, without noticeable improvement. Each patient was instructed
not to eat or drink for 24 hours before treatment. At the end of this
time, the patient was led to a lift where he found a table attractively
arranged with his most preferred foods. For the next 35 minutes, he
sat eating his dinner while the lift moved up and down. At the end
of the session, the patient was encouraged to take self-service lifts
in as many different buildings as possible. Both patients reported
little anxiety, and though one had a setback a little later on, he overcame it and both patients were still free of their fear at a two-year
follow up.

A fear of lifts seriously limits one's activities – especially in
America, where it is almost impossible to live or work without
using a lift. A Canadian immigrant, who has repeatedly asked his
English mother to visit him, cannot get her to do so because he lives
on the 12th floor and she would have to use the lift.

The claustrophobic's fear of being trapped or crowded in upon
has usually started after just such an experience. Sometimes it has
been more traumatic. One English mother of three, for instance,
said her claustrophobia 'may have originated from my husband's
attacks on me, for he always ended every argument with a beating,
and if I called for help, this was stopped by a pillow over my face,
or my being locked in a room'.

What is particularly striking, however, is the number of people
who have had really frightening experiences as children connected
with being locked in. One seventy-year-old woman said that 'when
I was a very small girl, if I was naughty my mother shut me in a
dark cupboard, the handle of which I could not reach. I understand
that a couple of times I was found unconscious on the floor of it;

other times I just screamed.' Another woman, also aged seventy, said that her mother, too, would shut her in the coal cupboard if she misbehaved. Again, 'there was no window and I couldn't undo the door as it was fastened on the outside'. A middle-aged woman similarly recalled being shut in the pantry as a punishment and being denied a light in her bedroom. And a Dutch girl set her phobia down to being thrown in a coal bunker by a woman who was looking after her while her mother was ill. 'I was shut in, no light, pitch black everywhere and choking in the coal dust, forgotten all day. I still shiver when I think about it. For years I could not be left alone and had nightmares galore.' The vogue for this type of punishment in the past was extraordinary, particularly in Victorian times. Yet even Silas Marner (written in 1861) had too much heart to shut Eppie in the coal hole for more than a minute or two.

Other vividly remembered childhood experiences usually concern hospitals. One phobic recalled her stay in hospital at the age of six, when chloroform was dripped onto a mask and she had to breathe this in while being held down. Exactly the same experience was shared by another woman, when she was a child of eight in hospital to have some teeth out. She, too, was held down while a mask was pressed on her face.

Many children who become claustrophobic have their first attack at school – in the main hall, or classroom, from which they cannot escape. One girl recalled her first experience at the age of eight: 'During assembly one morning, I felt strange and broke out into a hot sweat and my hearing was strange. I just had to get out of the hall. Much later, when I was at secondary school, I began to feel claustrophobic again. This only bothered me at assemblies and any other meeting which took place in the hall.' At college, the phobia returned.

Those who had attacks of claustrophobia at school could rarely give the reason for it, apart from the sudden panic feeling that they must at all costs get out of the classroom. But when claustrophobia was caused by even minor happenings in childhood, these incidents were remembered very clearly. In one case, an elderly woman recalled locking herself into a rather small bathroom and having a screaming fit till the door was forced open. Another recollected her fear during a game of 'Sardines' when about five girls were all pressed into one small cupboard. Many said that other school-children would lean against the door of the classroom they were in and refuse to let them out. One particularly remembered living in a village where the toilets were outside and older children would lock the younger ones in, for fun. Later on, as a teenager, she once managed to talk herself into overcoming her fear and going into a lift, but has not been able to repeat the experiment. Her fear was reinforced, later, after she and some others were trapped in the staff-room due to a jammed door, and firemen with axes had to get them out. ('Everyone else thought this was most amusing and I only managed to keep control by telling myself it would be possible to squeeze out of the tiny window.')

A forty-nine-year-old woman said that her claustrophobia had actually started when she got a dress stuck over her head when she was about six, and could hardly breathe. After this, she dodged a popular game played by her friends of capturing each other and shutting the victim in a garage shed. She also kept dreaming she was shut in somewhere, and on waking up invariably found herself right down the bed with all the sheets and blankets tightly over her head.

A dream can set off the phobia. A fifteen-year-old girl dreamed she was trapped in a red plastic lift and, from then on, dreaded going into lifts and has never gone into one alone in case it sticks between floors. Such anxiety dreams seem quite prevalent. One woman, who had gone down a water chute as a child and half suffocated, had recurrent dreams of either falling from a high cliff into water, or just sinking down in water. Only her wish to keep with the 'in group' at school, who went swimming, eventually enabled her to get into the swimming bath. However, her fears gradually spread: she became frightened of small dark rooms and always slept with the light on. On her first visit to the hairdressers, at twelve, the hairdryer reduced her to tears, and she had to get out of it.

Another woman remembered that when she had her hair washed as a child, 'I would scream and panic, struggling for air. My mother had to buy a large plastic hair-ring that stood out around my head rather like a halo.' Rather the same feelings were shared by another phobic who couldn't face having a hairdressers' gown around her neck, or indeed, wearing any high necklines. Acute family stress aggravated her feelings, and she then avoided lifts, crowded shops, and buses with self-closing doors. The same escalation happened with a seventeen-year-old girl, whose phobia started in a lift. 'I just couldn't breathe, and it got slowly worse. Now I cannot go in a lift; clean under a bed without moving it; go into a very small room; go under the stairs with a slanting roof; sleep with the window closed or on a top bunk; or with the sheets any higher than my neck and shoulders.'

It is this generalising of the fear that makes the claustrophobic's life so restrictive. Many of those I spoke to or heard from found it difficult to lead a normal life, as so many situations appeared to them to be claustrophobic. A young girl of sixteen, for instance, finds family holidays make her ill, as these are invariably spent in a caravan. And she is dreading the day when the language laboratory at her school is opened, when she will be expected to sit in one of the cubicles. And a seventy-year-old woman, whose favourite holiday had been taking coach trips, said: 'But now I cannot go unless I can be sure of being at the very front of the coach. I first felt this when in Edinburgh seven years ago, when getting in a coach to go round the city. We had to go nearly to the back and with a window close on one side of me, the seats in front being high, a friend on the other side, I suddenly felt I must get out. In a train, I am unhappy in a long coach, unless I can be in the aisle seat. Most public transport is a problem. Seats in the middle of a row at theatres are hopeless and any crowds, or where I feel hemmed in.' Another elderly woman had to turn down a council flat on the 10th floor: 'You can't trust the lifts in council property, they're always breaking down, so I couldn't take it, couldn't climb all those stairs.'

Sometimes phobics are immediately uneasy in any room where they can't see how to open the windows. One said, 'I can't bear being in a room with the curtains drawn and the doors shut. As for rooms with no windows, I would go raving mad if shut in one for five minutes. I can't stay down in large department stores with basement shopping for more than a few minutes: I have to go up to ground floor level or I would pass out.'

The same feeling of choking and smothering has affected another phobic now that she has moved from a larger house into a bungalow. She had always had claustrophobia, and had to sit near an open window, or at the end of a row in church, but now she finds she dislikes being in the bungalow in winter, when the doors and windows are shut, and the double glazing increases her feeling of being shut in. Her only relief is to go out of the room and walk about breathing deeply until her panic subsides.

A sense of suffocation beset one woman only after air-conditioning was introduced into trains, buses and buildings — because then there is no way of opening the windows. She also cannot look for long at ships in bottles without a feeling of smothering, and when taking an animal to the vet, puts it in a crate so that it has plenty of space to poke out its nose.

Another woman said that her claustrophobia only needed a small thing to spark it off. 'It could be some article of clothing that is a bit tight; bedding a bit too heavy; seeing or reading about anyone trapped in potholes or shut up in prison cells. I could never go through a narrow passage where I couldn't move my arms outwards. All my clothes are like sacks; I make them myself so as to get lots of room in the sleeves. Once, on holiday, I put on a new blouse which was tight in the sleeves. I tried to overcome the panic that rose within me. I couldn't get the blouse off because I'd come out in such a sweat that the material was stuck to my skin. So I hacked it off me in bits with the scissors. On my bed I only have two very light flannelette sheets on top — even in cold weather. If I feel any weight of bedding on top of me, I feel trapped. I never wear a nightie because they seem to get wrapped round my legs. Sometimes I've had to get up in the early hours of the morning when I get one of my "daren't sleep in bed" spasms. I've walked round and round trying to fight it, that terrible feeling of being shut in. It creates a blind, unreasonable panic. Both my sons have cars and would take me out, but to be shut up inside a car is sheer torture.'

Generally, claustrophobics neither like travelling in someone else's car, nor like to drive a car themselves. Their fear of being 'trapped inside' is the same as that felt by flying phobics, and is the prime factor in claustrophobia. Dr Alexandra Symonds, of the New York University College of Medicine, told me that, 'Women sometimes have a fear of driving because, symbolically, driving is taking charge of their life. It's a declaration: "I can't take care of myself, you have got to take care of me." The most common phobia I come across is fear of travelling. Some people are afraid of getting into a vehicle: one woman could only go if her husband was driving. People are afraid of their impulses.'

Being below ground level – whether in mines, submarines or underground trains – is also particularly feared. Some men, entering submarine service, find they cannot, in fact, cope with one of the recruitment tests – coming up from a small tank through many feet of water. And many phobics take the obvious way out, and, for example, avoid going in underground trains altogether. One elderly woman, who had stopped going by underground after her train had stopped for five minutes in a tunnel, now visits her sister weekly by bus – despite this journey taking three times as long. 'I think one needs reassurance,' she said. 'My daughter is a bit indifferent; she will say, "come on Mum, half the train journey is out in the open." But I know that if it stops underground, I get that awful feeling. My heart beats faster; I start to take my gloves off, my hat off and eventually I take my coat off and just sit there. I wouldn't scream; I wouldn't like to show myself up.'

When Dr Robert Sharpe, of the Centre for Behavioural Psychotherapy, London, was taking a claustrophobic along the street to the underground, he noticed the patient stamped his foot at the entrance, as a way of helping himself to allay anxiety. Dr Sharpe incorporated this into the patient's programme of 'anxiety management' – as a way of making him feel assertive while anxiety was going on. Instead of trying to curtail anxiety, this approach allows for it, even encourages it – and then patients are taught how to bring their anxiety under control. Their own methods for lowering anxiety – if any – are used. As far as the foot-stamping technique was concerned, the patient was first told to do this physically when anxious.

He was then told to do it only mentally – and later on even that was faded out. This way, he was able to control his anxiety whenever he felt it come on. And this is extremely important. For although the phobic might consider himself cured after overcoming his fears with the therapist present, he may panic on some future occasion. He will then start avoiding the situation again. As it is probable that panic *will* arise in certain situations – like an underground train stopping – it is essential that the phobic can control his panic sensations by certain techniques. If he once has confidence in his ability to control these sensations, then he is master of the situation.

As the claustrophobic's fear of being trapped is so strong, what happens in that most claustrophobic of all situations – being in prison? The psychiatrist at one of London's major prisons said she had never, in fact, come across a case of pure claustrophobia, although one of her colleagues in another prison had done so recently. 'It *could* be a means of curing it,' she said, 'as the situation rather resembles "flooding" in behaviour therapy treatment' (where the patient's anxiety hits top level, but cannot be maintained at this level, so subsides). The only difference is that there the patient always has to consent to being locked up.

Although it is understandable that one may become claustro-phobic in prison surroundings, it is a little surprising that so few genuine claustrophobics are admitted. But, 'You'll never find me breaking the law,' said one woman, 'no shoplifting, no nothing. My one dread is of being put inside: I just couldn't bear it.' So perhaps claustrophobia has the slender advantage of keeping its sufferers on the right side of the law!

9

Illness, Pain and Death

'My phobia about cancer began two years ago,' said a twenty-year-old girl, 'when I read the symptoms of a man who had died from it. I remember afterwards feeling very depressed. After a couple of days, this depression still persisted and I found myself dwelling more and more on it. This caused me to feel very tense, which resulted in a painful bust. My mother jokingly said, "I suppose you imagine you have breast cancer." It wasn't till then that I grasped onto this idea and coupled it with my own irrational anxiety. Then the nightmare began.'

She imagined that she was getting thinner and began constantly weighing herself. She wouldn't take her brassière off, feeling more secure with her breasts covered. Having a bath terrified her, as she knew the brassière would have to come off. She slept in it for months. She then read that if body moles enlarged or changed, it was a bad sign, so she continually looked at her moles and freckles and convinced herself that all sorts of things were happening to them. She got to the stage of dreading to have to go to work. If anyone mentioned the word cancer, or she saw it written down (even in the Cancer horoscope sign), she would be gripped with terror. Any pain she had she related to cancer, and she lay in bed imagining constant operations and death. Every whispered conversation she half heard, she related to the fact that someone had cancer – possibly herself.

Eventually, she couldn't stand it any longer and went to see her doctor and explained it all. He examined her and said there were no lumps and, for a while, she felt a new person and the discomfort disappeared. Then her fear crept back and she was put on tranquillisers. In her case, her fear varied in intensity, according to her emotional upheavals caused by work, family or boyfriends.

An illness phobia is a fear, in a perfectly healthy person, of a specific illness. In this way it differs from hypochondria, which is a more diffuse, general anxiety over health; and from paranoid delusion – for example, a fear of being poisoned. The kinds of illness people fear are usually those most currently prevalent, which nowadays are mainly cancer, venereal and heart disease (though syphilophobia is far from new, being extensively written about in medical literature from the seventeenth century onwards). In a study of 31 cases of cancer phobics, in 1948, J. A. Ryle found a large number of them had other psychiatric problems.

The causes for the phobia are varied. It may be that the phobic has identified with a relation or friend who has a certain illness; it may be psychologically caused (fears of V.D. due to guilt about sex); or because there is a known weakness in a part of the body. Publicity can generate a latent idea. After that given to the cancer operations undergone by Mrs Rockefeller and President Ford's wife, doctors' surgeries were inundated by frightened women (though only in a few did the fear irrationally persist).

As emotion and depression can play a large part, this complicates treatment. However, in one case of cancerophobia reported by W. D. Gentry, a woman was straightforwardly treated by first being relaxed and then, in imagination, having her breasts checked for cancer. This failed to decrease her anxiety over physical contact with her breasts and so treatment was then switched to actual breast stimulation, again while relaxed. She improved rapidly and was also taught to channel her mind away whenever she had obsessional thoughts of breast cancer.

One women I encountered goes one step further and physically runs away if she meets anyone who has had cancer. She will not go on a bus if she thinks a 'cancerous' person has also been on it; and will not use public toilets or telephones for the same reason. Since her butcher made the mistake of showing her a piece of liver with a growth on it, she won't go near his shop. And on finding out that the food shop next to the butcher's kept its cold meats in his deep freezer, she won't go in there, either.

Another cancerophobic finally overcame her fear, however, by facing up to it. She originally felt that any sign of illness pointed to cancer. Her doctor examined her and assured her she did not have cancer -- but cancerophobia. He gave her drugs and she completely forgot her fears while she was taking them -- but when she stopped these, she was as bad as ever. If she heard of anyone with cancer, she could actually feel pain in the same place as they had it. Her depression increased and she was unable to relax.

In the end, she decided pills were no good and it was up to her to take action or her life would be wrecked. For one thing her husband, who had been very understanding, was beginning to feel the strain, as she couldn't talk or think of anything else. So when she started to think about illness, she made herself think about something else, and if people talked about illness, she tried not to listen, or dwell on it. She knew her own weakness and that it was up to her to control it, as no one else could.

Few can act with such resolution, particularly if the fear has been with them for many years. One woman, in her early forties, had worried about her health since her teens, being very conscious of the fact that one relation had died of cancer at only thirty-four, and another had also gradually wasted away with it. She had not become phobic about cancer herself, however, until she married in her mid-thirties. Her marriage was not a happy one -- her husband knocked her around and would deliberately upset her by referring to her fear. She thought her phobia probably stemmed from the unhappy state she was in. She had admittedly had some cause for alarm. After constantly going to the doctor, he arranged for her to have a breast cancer test to set her mind at rest. A fortnight later, when she went back for the result, she was told that she had to go for a further test. Finally she was admitted to hospital for an operation. A young doctor there frightened her even more by saying that if they were certain she didn't have cancer, they wouldn't be operating. It turned out, in fact, that she just had fibrous tissues. She then worried that these would turn into cancer.

Since leaving hospital, this woman's fears about cancer have become even more obsessive and she is convinced it is about to strike her somewhere. If she gets a spot and it will not go, she is round at the doctor's immediately. 'Once a scar came up into a little lump and the sister at the health centre said, if it doesn't go, see your doctor. I was so panic-stricken, I ran out and left my coat on the seat. I also worried about my leg, as one of the bones stuck out. Then someone at work said, "I know a little boy who had a lump come up on his knee and he has had an X-ray and it's cancer." I said, "Oh my God," and went back to the office shaking like a leaf. I sat down and deep breathed, and if I'd have been alone I would have screamed until I was hoarse. I had an X-ray, and was told it was nothing, so was reassured.

'Every little ache and pain, I know it's cancer. It's imprinted across my brain and the harder I try not to worry, the worse I get. One little thing and I just flip and rush round to the doctor. For instance, I gave up smoking five or six years ago, but took it up again recently and started to get a pain in my back. I was sure I had given myself cancer, and yet I had only had three packets of cigarettes. People say, why are you like it? But I just feel it would shatter me if I had cancer. In my mind, an operation would never be successful, as I would expect it to turn up somewhere else. Dying doesn't worry me; it's the actual thought of cancer.'

Another rather emotionally disturbed girl, who had refused to go to school from the age of thirteen through fear of sickness, developed a phobia about leukaemia when she was fifteen – after a family friend had died of this at the age of seventeen. This fear lasted for about five years, and she insisted that her parents took her to the local doctor for regular blood checks. She then married when she was in her early twenties and became pregnant. This temporarily ended her phobia, as she felt she could not become pregnant if she had a serious disease. Her marriage turned out to be a disaster, and she became ill with fever, loss of weight and sickness. She went for stomach X-rays, and was finally told she had an 'irritable bowel syndrome'. This failed to alleviate her certainty that she had cancer; and she has now taken to drinking quite a lot, not getting up till 1 p.m. every day, and living like a vegetable.

People can also get a phobia about medical apparatus. In one case in Canada, for example, reported by Professor F. J. Jarrett, a thirty-six-year-old married woman had a fear of having her blood pressure taken. The fear had spread to other connected situations, such as being in a doctor's office; reading the words 'blood pressure'; or hearing about someone with heart disease. The phobia had started after she became anxious about her health when first pregnant. During her second pregnancy she became hypertense and much attention was paid to the level of her blood pressure. She was quite ill after the birth. Her third pregnancy and delivery were without complications, but she developed an increasing fear of any situation connected with blood pressure. She would not have a fourth child as this would mean her blood pressure had to be taken. She and her husband decided to adopt a child, but on finding that adoption regulations required a blood pressure test, she postponed the application. She finally had it taken, but only with great distress.

The phobia affected her in various ways. She had to leave any group which began talking about illness connected with blood pressure or the heart and she wouldn't go to the doctor, even when quite ill. Her husband would censor magazines and papers in case there was any mention of blood pressure or heart disease.

The treatment used was a new form of aversion relief therapy. She listed the situations she feared, starting with the least fearful and ending with the most feared. In that order, these were:

1 Card with 'blood pressure' written on it in small letters.
2 Card with 'blood pressure' written on it in large letters.
3 Seeing blood pressure armband three feet away.
4 Seeing therapist holding armband.
5 Seeing therapist roll armband up.
6 Seeing therapist inflate armband.
7 Taking armband from therapist and handing it back immediately.

8 Taking armband, changing it to other hand, handing it back.
9 Holding armband and inflating it.
10 Armband placed on arm.
11 Armband on arm and inflated.
12 Having blood pressure taken.

She was then asked to breathe in, then breathe out fully and then hold her breath by placing her hand over her mouth and pinching her nose. She was told to hold her breath as long as she possibly could. At the point of breathing in again, the first item on the list – the card – was held up. When she no longer felt tension, the next higher was presented. The reasoning behind this treatment is that as the patient takes a gulp of air, after holding her breath, her relief causes her tension to evaporate – and it is difficult to summon it up again when immediately faced with a feared object.

The treatment, in this case, proved most successful. By the ninth weekly session, she was able to have her blood pressure taken on both arms and in various rooms without any discomfort. She could also handle the apparatus and take her own blood pressure. At the follow-up a month later, she reported she had gone to her own doctor for a routine medical check up for the first time in ten years.

Having one's blood pressure taken is a standard part of medical procedure; so is having an injection. In certain circumstances, refusal to have either of these done could result in death. Some people with phobias about injections told me that they knew this, and were prepared to die rather than be injected. In one case, involving an infection, this nearly happened.

The girl concerned said that she remembered avoiding injections at school, possibly due to some painful ones she had had in hospital when she was six years old. At fifteen she met (and later married) a boy who was a main-line drug addict. At that point, her fear really came out. When needles were about, she 'shrank, screamed and shouted'. The marriage broke up, and 15 months later she became pregnant by another man. She intended to have an abortion, and went along for a medical test. The sister told her to roll her sleeve up for an injection, but the girl refused – despite being told that she would have to have one somewhere along the line, or she would die. ('I thought, in that case, I better rush out and cash in my premium bonds.')

This decided her to have the baby, on the ground that if women in the jungle could have them without injections, so could she. All through her pregnancy, however, the subject came up. ('Whoever I encountered said, "It's only a little prick, it won't hurt". People think it's a matter of being strong, but it's a different part of the mind.') She had an easy labour, but at the end was told she would have to be stitched. Again, she refused an injection, though the doctor stormed at her and the midwife walked out. To avoid injection, packs were used – though this was a long process.

She was seen by a hospital psychiatrist, who persuaded her to take treatment ('it consisted of lying on a couch and talking'). Then she moved and went for further treatment to Claybury Hospital, where she saw Brian Wijesinghe, the Principal Psychologist. She did some I.Q. tests, completed some questionnaires, and started going weekly for about an hour. At first, she just sat and talked to him, without needles being mentioned. Then, after a few weeks, he asked her to think of a hypodermic needle and imagine it getting closer. He asked how she felt and what she was thinking of – saying she was 90 per cent there if she could imagine it mentally. It was rather too soon for her – she panicked and wanted to leave. He did not realise how deep-seated her phobia was. At this stage treatment was switched from imagining needles to talking about her childhood, marriage and relationships. She began to understand some of the reasons for her phobia and realised that her overcharged emotions as a child had to find an outlet.

After several months, she was asked to try holding a needle to see her reaction. Each week following she got a bit further. The next time, she touched herself with it; and the week after she was touched with it; then it was slipped under the skin of the thumb, and then under the skin of her arm. Finally the ward sister was called in to inject her with distilled water. At that stage, her personal life took a turn for the worse. She had to be treated for depression and could not cope with needles as well. Recovering, she took up the treatment again. She was given a hypodermic needle to keep in a drawer at home, and managed to hold it, which at one time she could not do. She is now able to have injections outside the treatment setting and has been injected by her own G.P. and the dentist.

A dental phobia can also be quite dangerous to the person concerned as instead of just disliking to visit the dentist, the phobic will allow his or her teeth to rot away rather than do so. One woman explained the effect it had had on her:

'At the age of twelve, my eye teeth came through very crooked and high up in the gum. I remember my mother dragging me along to the dentist and both of them standing behind me saying I would have to go into hospital to have them out, or alternatively that if left alone they might straighten themselves out. After that I would make up any excuse to get out of going as I knew darned well that they would never straighten out on their own. I managed to bluff my way through school and it was such a relief when I actually left as I knew no school dentist could come round wondering why I hadn't kept an appointment. Also, when I was at school we were always given a note asking us whether we would like to use the school dentist or the family one, and I always managed to forge my mother's signature stating the latter.

'For the next ten years my life was unbearable. Looking back on it now, I honestly didn't know how I didn't go off my head. I loved going out with boys, but most of them must have thought I was very shy or a miserable person: I could never laugh in public, only half smile and bow my head. I could never relax, not even for a minute. Parties were unbearable, especially when someone told me a joke. And worst of all was the fact that I knew I would have to go to the dentist sometime in the future. As the years went by, my teeth got worse and I became more withdrawn. When I was twenty I did meet someone and I knew if anyone would understand it would be him, but I still could not bring myself to tell him and on I went with my head bowed down and all the time thinking that I mustn't open my mouth too much and knowing that I had to go to the dentist in the end.

'We became engaged on my twenty-first birthday and a year later we got married. You can imagine my wedding day was unbearable for me. The wedding photos were a nightmare, with the photographers asking me to put my head up and smile, and the whole time I was in a cold sweat. Anyway, we moved to the south coast, my husband got a good job and I could stay at home and not talk to anyone, so therefore I didn't have to open my mouth at all. Then I became pregnant and of course I was petrified I would have a full medical check-up and would have to open my mouth. I told my husband that I had been to the doctor, but at seven months I was afraid that by not going I might endanger the baby, so eventually I went and as luck would have it, nobody even bothered to look.

'So my son was born and it was wonderful. While he was small my whole life changed. As a baby he didn't know what teeth were and I could smile and laugh at him all day long. As I had never laughed, my face used to ache at the end of the day, but it was worth it. But all this time my phobia was growing, the teeth were getting worse and my son was getting older. Children are very honest and I knew the time would come when I couldn't laugh with him any more and this upset me more than anything. When he was two and a half we had our second child. And again laughing with her was wonderful, but I knew it couldn't last.

'I had always wondered when my husband went to the dentist why he never mentioned that I never went, but I certainly wasn't going to. Every night I would lie in a cold sweat thinking about it and as my son got older I knew I had to do something. Each night got worse; I couldn't sleep, I would wait until my husband was asleep and go downstairs and cry my eyes out. I honestly thought I was going mad. On one of my bad nights my husband came down and I was in such a state that I managed to blurt the whole lot out. In the morning he got up and went to work and I thought that he would just accept the fact and wait until I was ready. However, he came back at lunch time and said that he had had a long talk to the dentist and he understood how I felt and would see me the next day That afternoon, and until 10.45 the next day, was unbearable. I was sick, I had diarrhoea, I had a temperature and I certainly didn't sleep a wink. I took four tranquillisers that night and six the next morning and in the end my husband had to practically carry me in. I'm not sure whether I was afraid of what he would do or what he would think of my teeth and, worst of all, what he would think of me. Anyway, he told me I had left it so long that the roots were all twisted and that the front six teeth would have to come out. I still had about seven other fillings that needed doing and I knew if I wanted the front ones done, it would be no good not turning up for the other treatment. Each visit was a nightmare. Every time I went my husband had to take hours off work, as if he hadn't been there I certainly wouldn't have turned up.

'Eventually the dentist said that on the next visit he would take out the front six. My husband took the day off and we went together. I had gas and it was all over in a few seconds. I managed to get to the car and just sat there and my husband handed me a present. A mirror. At first I was too afraid to look, but when I did I couldn't believe how radiant I looked. But I will never get over my phobia. In fact I am ashamed to admit I have not been back to the dentist since that last visit. I will walk half a mile out of my way rather than pass the door, in case he sees me.'

One explanation for a fear of going to the dentist is the possibility of having to have gas and therefore losing consciousness – a primitive but widely shared fear. In *Studies in Personality*, W. E. Rivers cites a case of a patient whose fear of fainting, and thus losing consciousness, was really a fear of death – although this was buried so deep in the patient's subconscious that she hadn't realised it herself. Her fear of death dated from a previously unremembered episode when she was eight years old and had been frightened by the death of a pet animal. Since then, a fear of death had been with her almost constantly, though not always consciously.

According to Freud, death is symbolised in dreams by departure, like a train journey. It can, however, be more straightforwardly represented, as in dreams about funerals. One woman told me her nightmares were always about cremation – about which she had a great sense of horror of reading, hearing or speaking, even though she had never been to one. She couldn't understand why she had this fear. A specific incident triggered off death phobia in another girl when she was in her mid-twenties. Now, 20 years later, it has become more intense. ('Indeed, my fear of death has become so real to me that it amazes me that it has not actually happened, as I've been in such a state of fear that I certainly thought my heart would have given out.')

In her case, what originally happened was that while her mother was in hospital, her father died quite unexpectedly. This shocked her, but it wasn't until two months after her father's funeral that the phobia about death started. 'We moved house to try and occupy my mind with something different. Then, on my twenty-eighth birthday, I was playing a record when suddenly this fear came over me that I was about to die there and then. I once again ran out of the house in fear and walked up and down the street wringing my hands and praying to God not to let me die.' She is frightened to go to sleep at night, but feels there is nothing anyone can do: 'the fear of death is still there.' (This fear of death is different from the *sensation* of death, which might come, for instance, during a severe chest pain.)

J. Wolpe, in 1961, treated a phobia about death by means of relaxation combined with the patient imagining the situations she feared. These situations, in increasing order of anxiety, were:

1 Driving past a cemetery (the nearer, the more disturbing).
2 The sight of a dead animal.
3 Seeing a funeral procession (the nearer, the more disturbing).
4 The word 'death'.
5 Being at a house of mourning.
6 Being at a burial.

Only after the patient could imagine the first situation, and remain relaxed, was the second one presented, and so on – until she was finally able to imagine all six situations calmly. The patient can, of course, also be taken to real-life situations, such as to the undertaker, or an actual funeral.

Phobics quell their anxiety by trying to avoid what they fear: cat phobics will cross the road if they see a cat; plane phobics will not fly. But those with a phobia about death or illness cannot get away from their fear. As Milton says, they 'live a life half death, a living death'.

10

Rare Phobias

Robert Benchley once confessed to suffering from 'kneebophobia' — a fear of the knees suddenly bending the wrong way. This particular phobia is not included in the *Dunlop Book of Facts* – even though this lists over 150 different phobias. Many of these are well known, like claustrophobia; others, less familiar, are understandable – such as fear of work (ergasiophobia). But there are also some stranger phobias: indeed, almost any object frightens someone. There is, for example, the fear of sacred things (hierophobia); of home surroundings (ecophobia); of string (linonophobia); of oneself (autophobia). The list of phobias at the end of the book gives further examples.

People can also have an irrational fear of certain situations occurring. One can be, for instance, phobic about being beaten (rhabdophobia), bound (merintophobia) or buried alive (taphophobia). And ordinary social situations can be equally disturbing, like a fear of thirteen people around the table (triskaidekaphobia), touching or being touched (haphephobia), and making physical love (erotophobia).

Some of the listed phobias would cause immense complications in the life of anyone suffering from them. How do you cope if you have a phobia about standing upright (stasiphobia), or gaiety (cherophobia), or going to bed (clinophobia), or responsibility (hypnegiaphobia), or sitting idle (thessophobia)? On the other hand, some might act as a useful built-in conscience – such as a fear of making false statements (mythophobia), or neglecting a duty (paralipophobia).

Because the more bizarre phobias border on the ludicrous, the phobic conceals his fear – believing it would provoke amazed laughter rather than sympathy. The varieties of fear are really surprising, as some of the following comments I received show:

'My fear is of churches; I even have nightmares about them. Nothing will stop me being frightened of them, especially at night, or if you don't know that they are there.'

'My phobia is the sight of canal locks. When I was four or five, a bigger lad said to me, when walking near one, how would you like to fall down there? Ever since, I'll walk miles out of my way just to avoid going by one. I came across one by accident the other day, and I couldn't move; I just stood there and sweated and shivered. Everyone wanted to know what was wrong and I just couldn't tell them. But my wife, who knows about it, dragged me back out of sight of it and then I was all right again.'

'Mine is a fear of dolls. They terrify me, especially the eyes. And this also applies to tailors' dummies, ventriloquists' dolls.'

'I have a phobia about anyone touching my neck: I even scream if my husband puts his hands on my cheek, in fun.'

'My fear is of looking in a mirror, or in any reflective surfaces. At college some months ago, I was grabbed from behind and jokingly told I needed a shave [a girl speaking]. I have since had a hair-line removed by electrolysis, but neither this nor sedatives has cured me. I am anxious to return to my studies but this situation is keeping me almost bed bound.'

'I have a phobia about traffic lights. Confronted with them, I just die and cannot move one foot before the other; and will go the longer way around to avoid them.'

'I have a morbid fear of ships. If ever there is a disaster at sea and it appears in pictures in the newspapers, I avoid buying them. A few months ago, a car firm used a ship in an advert. I was eating my breakfast the day it appeared and I literally nearly died of fright; it caught me unawares as I was thumbing through the paper.'

'I fear all things under water, such as groyne parts, pier structures, sides of wharfs, harbours and the under part of bridges.'

'My little girl of seven and a half has a horror of buttons. She was able to make us understand this fear when she was eighteen months. We go through tears and recrimination every time she has to wear a buttoned garment.'

'Since childhood, I've had a fear of homemade cakes, biscuits or pastries – though shop and factory-made ones are perfectly acceptable. Perhaps it is because my father used to dislike the old lady living next door and would make an issue about never touching anything she had baked.'

'I cannot bear to see a mass of pips. I can't cut open a melon, tomatoes, peppers or marrows, without my skin crawling and having to drop the knife and leave the kitchen. I think it is due to having seen a crawling mass of maggots when I was a child.'

'My fear is of cold weather and below freezing temperatures. When I get this feeling of panic, I sweat heavily and this makes me even more frightened as I worry that sweating heavily at below-freezing temperatures will eventually do me some physical injury. Since I have had this problem, I avoid going out when the weather is really cold and often spend several weeks off work in winter.'

'I have an overwhelming fear of doctors. When I was pregnant, the doctor always said, "your blood pressure is up". But I always thought this was due to my fear of him.'

'Since my early teens, I have suffered badly when people are coughing: I feel mentally so distressed, as though I had been doing all the coughing myself.'

'I have always been afraid of walking under or near trees: I nearly always get the feeling they are going to fall on me.'

'As far back as a young girl, I have had an inward fear about eyes. Due to ill-health, I used to have very dark circles and my left eye often swelled up. Now, even if I see a person rubbing or squinting their eyes, my whole body revolts; and when operations are spoken about concerning the eyes, or I see them on television or in a film, I want to be quite ill.'

'I have a fear of foam baths. I could not bring myself to step into a bubble bath; I must be able to see the water clearly. I also have a fear of the cold; I cannot watch butchers or fishmongers cutting up and handling meat or fish in cold weather; and if, when passing a canal or river, I imagine someone falling in the freezing water, I feel so ill I nearly faint. I can't bear to see anyone cleaning a step on a frosty morning.'

Strange though the above fears and phobias are, perhaps one of the strangest was Sir Richard Burton's fear of honey. In his biography, his wife said that he 'could not sit in the room with honey and knew even if it was kept in the most secret drawer or cupboard'.

All phobics – whether their phobia is common or uncommon – practise various strategies to avoid the situation they fear. A good example of the type of precaution taken appeared in the obituary of a *New Yorker* cartoonist, who died in 1974: 'Dunn suffered the burden of several phobias, the most intense of which was a fear of fire. On a few occasions when he planned to visit a friend in an apartment building new to him, he went so far as to secure copies of the blueprints of the building and ascertain the position of its fire escapes. During the past ten or twelve years he enjoyed many happy times in a club in midtown that had, for him, the cardinal advantage of possessing a broad flight of stairs leading down to the street. At monthly meetings, he would stroll about sipping a Martini and chatting animatedly with friends, at the same time keeping an eye on the front door.'

An American girl of twenty-five, whose fear of fire started at the age of two (when she became hysterical if a pot boiled over), always avoids the situation. She ruins family picnics by not getting out of the car if she sees people cooking on open camp-fires; and, in high school, her home economics teacher failed her for refusing to light an oven. (Even now she won't do this.) She checks the gas fire in her flat before going to bed, though dreams of fire still wake her. Her preoccupation with fire, however, tempts her into reading about witches being burned at the stake, and to revisit films like *Joan of Arc* and *The Devils* where such scenes exist – even though it makes her feel physically sick. This fascination extends to real life: when a car she was travelling in burst into flames, she sat and stared at these and had to be dragged out. Strangely, though she will not use a cigarette lighter, she is unbothered by matches. (A 'match' phobic who lives in Britain, on the other hand, has a deep feeling of horror and disgust at the idea of actually touching a box of matches, or of having them anywhere near him at all.)

A fear of water can be even more complicated to live with than a fear of fire. One housewife panics if even baths her child; she herself has to have a strip wash only. Another cannot bear rivers or pools – the sea especially – and if she takes her children to the sea, has to sit far away from it, facing the other way. She recalls the worst episode of her life as being her total immersion in water, when becoming a Baptist.

One Scotswoman recalled that when, in her teens, she unexpectedly saw a bath, basin, sink or lavatory full to the brim with water, she was terror-struck. She then remembered an incident at the age of eighteen months when she turned on the hot tap of a handbasin and stood beside it until it overflowed, scalding her severely. Once she realised the cause of the phobia, she overcame it.

Knowing the reason, however, does not mean an automatic cure. One of the water phobics, who could not wash her hair when alone in the house and was also afraid of getting water on her feet, attributed it to her mother's warning that to wash her hair when unwell, or get her feet wet, 'turns you funny'. Her doctor suggested she deliberately tried doing it, as it would then go; but though she tried running a bath, she couldn't manage to get in.

Other phobics, who remember their fear starting in childhood, are still affected by it. A fish phobic, whose fear started after some children put a fish down the neck of her dress, where it flopped about until it died, said: 'I go rigid if I am in a room with a fish tank and I couldn't touch a fish to save my life. I cannot even watch fish on television or at the cinema and I have never learned to swim in case I meet a fish in the water. My family accept it and if ever they want fish for a meal, they deal with it themselves. My children have never had goldfish as pets and my son has never gone fishing, all because of me.' The same sort of incident triggered off a phobia of frogs in another woman.

In a slightly stranger case, a woman, when about three years old, had a near fatal illness which left her with a distinct memory of having floated over the world, looking down. Up to the age of fourteen, she had a recurrent nightmare about the size of infinity and the universe. The result was a lack of scale, a fear of maps. 'I used to tear out pictures from the children's encyclopaedia of "How the world began". If I open a map of the Himalayas, to me they are as big as if I was hovering over them and the features of the country-side show up as if I could see them all. My hands sweat all over. Some eighteenth-century travellers used to hate mountains, too; Defoe called them "revolting". It was a late development to like them at all. But there are certainly maps in the drawer which I wouldn't touch. An inch map of, say, Northumberland, would be very alarming. I either take the map outside, if I have to look at it, as I'm not afraid in the garden; or else I take a dash at it.'

I came across about a dozen people suffering from balloon phobia. One of them said that she knew how ridiculous her fear was: 'But if I am in a room with an inflated balloon, I become sick, giddy and if I don't leave the room at once I faint. I am lucky that most places only have balloons up at Christmas and the New Year. But parties are a nightmare, as I have two small children and they go to parties and play with balloons.' She doesn't remember being afraid of balloons until she was in her late teens, when a relative squeezed a balloon until it burst. She remembers leaving the room and putting her fingers in her ears so as not to hear the bang. Since then, balloons have horrified her.

A girl of twenty-three who said that she, too, could not bear to touch a balloon or even have one near her, said her fear began when she was a child, when her father would blow up balloons and get pleasure from bursting them behind her back. She also rather dreads Christmas: 'Last Christmas, one of the guests at our Christmas party found out about my phobia and chased me round our house with a balloon threatening to burst it. I ran and locked myself in our bathroom for an hour, shaking – much to the amazement of the other guests. I would rather have jumped off a cliff than have that balloon burst near me.' Her experience was echoed by another woman who, on one occasion, actually knocked herself unconscious in a hysterical attempt to get out of a ballroom on New Year's Eve, when she was caught unawares by balloons floating down from the ceiling. The touch of the rubber also revolts her – and the others – though the noise of them being burst or 'pulled around' is rated worst.

Unless it seriously interferes with their lives – which is unlikely except at Christmas – balloon phobics rarely apply for treatment. One twenty-seven-year-old man did so (in a case reported by J. P. Watson and colleagues in 1971) when he became engaged and knew he might be faced with balloons in the forthcoming parties. He had been phobic since the age of seven. During treatment, he was encouraged to approach the balloon as closely and quickly as he could manage, and stay there until his anxiety lessened. His attempts to avoid it – such as turning his head or eyes away, and withdrawing his hand – were discouraged. By the end session, he was able to tolerate about 90 balloons being blown up and burst around his head.

Another unusual fear was that of packing suitcases. This started gradually in childhood, and was tied up with leaving the protection of home. But even after getting married, the phobic made excuses not to go away with her husband on holidays or business, as this brought on nightmares of school packing, and made her ill.

A more minor fear of creeper plants also set in at the age of eleven or twelve in another woman's case. It started after she had to go through a tunnel of creepers in a wood, to get to a clearing. She tripped on one of them, became panic stricken, and was hysterical by the time she got out, imagining they were going to wrap themselves around her. She still will not go near them or pass plants like old man's beard. The fear has spread to roots and even pulling out ground elder makes her come out in a sweat. One girl's rather similar fear of nettles was compounded, when she was fourteen, by her father forcing her to go through some dense, tall nettles, in an (unsuccessful) attempt to cure her.

Some of these more unusual phobias, although starting in childhood, seem to have begun for no apparent reason. Why should a child in a pram scream whenever it was taken into a store with department signs hanging from the ceiling by cords; and, as an older child, not be able to bear seeing children on swings in parks? And why should this last into adulthood, causing the person concerned, for example, to leave a restaurant which had swinging lights? Why, too, should a child run away screaming when a favourite aunt turns up wearing pale pink? Or, when in hospital, aged six, be perfectly all right in a side ward, painted green, but when transferred to the main ward, painted pale pink, run a high temperature and refuse to eat? Even today, as a grandmother, this woman cannot stand pale pink: 'To look at it makes me feel really ill, the whole area moves in a sickening way, like a mass of maggots.'

. However, some of these stranger phobias can be put down to straightforward incidents, occurring when the person was an adult, but having a much greater after-effect than normal. For instance, one woman, after seeing the scene in *Odette* where Odette's fingernails are going to be pulled out, cannot, 20 years later, bear to see anyone cut their nails in front of her. 'It makes me go hot and clammy and my tummy starts churning and I feel really ill; almost like fainting. My husband always does it in front of me to try to make me overcome the feelings, but I have to go out of the room. No one, only myself, knows the agony I go through and I must say that no one believes me when I tell them: they just laugh.' One student's horror of libraries comes from the fact that an extremely unhappy year, working in a library, ended in a breakdown. And a latent dislike of mud turned into a phobia after a woman walked into a deep muddy ditch; in her panic to get out, she left both boots stuck in three feet of mud. Now, even if she watches a television programme showing the characters walking ankle deep in mud, she feels sick and shaky.

After moving from a downstairs flat into an upstairs one, one housewife now has a fear of 'weight'. She explained it by saying that it was taking all that heavy furniture – a fridge, stove – upstairs. She feels that everything is too heavy, like lorries and buildings, and that the ground can't hold all the weight: 'Even at work I think about it, or when I do washing and the clothes are all heavy with water. Even when I am having a bath, I think the bathful of water is too heavy.'

Most of these phobics haven't tried any form of treatment; few even admit their fears. Understandably. Children, once knowing another child's fear, will often cruelly tease him; given a really unusual phobia, adults will behave in precisely the same way. ('You're not *really* afraid of maps, are you? Come and look at this one.') There's no understanding: just curiosity, slight sadism, and amused disbelief.

I I

Obsessions

'It started when I was working very hard on a design project; my workshop was a double garage and I was phobic about people breaking in. I would lock the workshop up at night, but I lacked the confidence I was doing it properly. It was quite common for me to take as long as 2 hours to lock up and turn the lights off and make sure nothing was going to catch fire; that the windows were shut, box lids on, and doors locked. I especially had to check and recheck that the doors were locked. On one occasion, when I stopped work at sunset, my wife and I spent the entire night locking up.

'I used to write notes to remind myself to do a particular job, so in my mind there was a real risk that one of these notes might go out of the window or door; so after locking up, I would look all round to see there was nothing lying around. I used to worry about how far these documents might have blown. My fear was that if one of these papers blew away, this would cause a fatality to the person carrying out my design project. I felt I was only doing my job properly if I kept my documents. I found it difficult to walk along the street, as every time I saw paper, I wondered if it was some of mine. I had to pick it all up, unless it was brown chocolate paper, or lined paper, which I didn't use. And before I got on my bike, I checked that nothing was sticking out of my pocket and got my wife to recheck. She was very patient. I would have to sit in a certain seat on the bus so that, when I walked downstairs, I could look back up and check no papers were left on the seat. I couldn't smoke a cigarette without taking it to bits and checking there was no document between the paper and tobacco. I couldn't even have sex because I thought a piece of paper might get intertwined into the mattress. I could do nothing that would cause the loss or destruction of a document; and in the hottest summer, the windows had to be made absolutely airtight in case a document blew out. I was only working on the project part-time at one point and when I arrived at my office job, I used to go into the gents and check through my entire pockets, so that I knew that everything on my desk was the firm's property only and there was no chance of getting the two muddled up.'

His obsessions worsened, to the point when he had to spend a year or so in a psychiatric hospital. They still preoccupy him today.

There is disagreement over whether obsessional fears are the same as phobic ones: most psychiatrists consider this is not the case. Unlike phobics, obsessives do not fear an actual object or situation. They fear its *consequences*. The fear of the man just quoted was not of losing paper, but of what would happen if he did. The only way to prevent these unnameable consequences, to the obsessive's way of thinking, is by carrying out protective rituals.

Most of us have practised 'magic' rituals or compulsive acts — like touching a certain tree on the way to school, or not treading on the lines on the pavement; and, in some cases, these are carried through to adulthood. Those who have an obsessive personality, or obsessive traits, tend to be orderly, perfectionistic, stubborn and dislike ambiguity and uncertainty: they want order in their work, their home surroundings, in what they wear. They may not have particular compulsions, but they like (or insist on) things being done the right way. This could be viewed as a personality disorder. However, those people with obsessive-compulsive reactions (estimated at 1 to 2 per cent of all psychiatric patients in Britain and America) feel *compelled* to carry out certain ritual acts — such as washing their hands ten times — as a placatory act in order to ward off unspecified but impending 'doom'. Obsessions are intrusive ideas or thoughts which the person cannot rid himself of, despite knowing they are unreasonable; compulsions are the actions which result from the thoughts.

These acts or rituals, as Leon Salzman says in his book, *The Obsessive Personality*, 'are required to cope with potential dangers, and if changed or interrupted will result in severe anxiety.' This is because these acts are carried out to *alleviate* anxiety – possibly about some repressed past act or misconduct. The compulsive acts only temporarily end the anxiety, which builds up again, leading to a repetition of the act.

Compulsive rituals are enormously time-consuming. One woman, for instance, has to wash her hands in a certain way after touching 'unclean' objects – namely, from fingers to wrist, from wrist to elbow, and from elbow to upper arm – and then repeat the performance until her anxiety is over, which could be several times. Hands can become painfully raw this way. Another young girl has to wash in a certain order when she has a bath. 'And also when I wash clothes or clean anything – floor, carpet, windows and so on – I have to clean them in a certain manner to make sure I do not miss any. I can never hurry because I would not feel that it has been done properly.' One man, with a fear of 'contamination' from outside getting inside his house, has to wash the flight of steps down which he walks each night. On going inside, he has to remove his outdoor contaminated clothes and change into 'clean' ones, then have a bath. This takes up half the evening.

The most common compulsive ritual act is constant hand-washing. The obsessive fear here is one of germs and contamination. One woman said: 'Ever since childhood, whatever I do, wherever I go, always in my mind is a fear of germs. It is part of the way I am. When I was about nine years old, I developed a habit of licking my hands all the time. This, I felt, was a way to make sure they were clean, because although I don't fear germs for *myself*, I fear I may pass them on to someone else. My parents took me to a psychiatrist, but I was very ashamed of my fear and didn't tell him about it. So my licking of hands was put down to the fact that my mother was pregnant and that I was over-anxious about it.

'The years went by, and sometimes it was worse than other times.

I remember in my teens spending so long in the toilet that I was constantly being told off. I'm now married and expecting a baby. When I learnt this, I decided to seek medical help. Words cannot explain the embarrassment I went through explaining to my doctor. Fortunately he was very understanding and put me in touch with a psychiatrist. I have now seen this psychiatrist twice; so far he has only asked questions about myself. I did hope he could cure me in months by some miracle, but the last time I saw him, he told me to come back in three months' time, when I'll be seven months pregnant. That is three months of worrying, disinfecting this, that and the other, making my hands and arms sore through washing.'

This woman could give no explanation as to why she should have started to fear germs as a child, and several psychotherapists mentioned that obsessives resist attempts to delve too deeply into possible reasons for the onset of their behaviour. (One said firmly that all his obsessional hand-washers 'had sex guilt'.) The 'guilt' explanation for handwashing one's sins away has been standard ever since Pontius Pilate. A more likely one is that it is usual for parents to punish children for getting dirty, and washing hands is a way of mollifying parents' anger. It could therefore become a way of relieving fear – and be used in other situations associated with dirt.

One or two of those I encountered with washing rituals were quite clear as to why their fears had started. One girl of twenty-one said: 'Both my parents were from poor families and my three sisters and myself were brought up, till I was eight, in very small, cramped accommodation in some of the worse parts of London. Although my mother always kept us clean and as neat as possible, under such bad conditions, I always feel that my thing about cleanliness stems from there. At one point in our lives we had a council flat for two weeks – it was like a dream come true. Then suddenly, what should appear but bugs. Apparently, the previous tenants had been so filthy, it had been a perfect breeding ground. At one time we had nowhere to live, and were promptly plonked in a rest centre in Hackney. The filth of people there was astounding. We bathed at least twice a day for fear of lice. Everything of this kind throughout my life has left its mark. I have cleaning rituals which must be performed every day. Every inch of my body must be cleaned thoroughly and my hair every two days. These rituals are necessary to my whole being, but, at the same time, drive me up the wall. Even tatty old jeans are thoroughly washed and pressed every time I wear them.'

In another case, the reason was equally clear cut. One morning, when travelling to work in a friend's car, a young man was asked to hold a very small puppy, which during the journey wetted on his hand. He had read somewhere that dog urine caused infection and, on arriving at the office, pumice-stoned the part of his hand the dog had soiled until it was almost raw.

From that day onwards he developed a fear of getting his hands dirty and would wash them after touching anything at all. He would not open a door with his hands, but manipulated the door handle with his wrist – first taking care to pull his shirt down over his wrist so that no part of his skin touched the door knob. He invested in gallon tins of disinfectant, which were kept in the bathroom and kitchen, and though he had been an enthusiastic gardener, he now neglected the garden as he wouldn't touch the rake or spade. He became increasingly fanatical about germs and bugs. On one occasion, his wife placed the clean laundry on the arm of the settee in the living room, prior to taking it up to the linen cupboard. As soon as he saw this, he put the whole lot in the dustbin, saying that it was now covered with germs from the settee.

His wife became frantic about his behaviour, which lasted until he went into the Navy in the last war. There, the thing which apparently impressed him was the cleanliness of everything. He stayed in the Navy throughout the war and, though still a stickler for hygiene on return, was not obsessionally so.

Obsessional thoughts and ruminations can also disrupt one's life. One man, for example, had a fear of giving vent to aggressive or sexual impulses, and the temptation to yell obscene words. These thoughts occupied almost all his waking time – coming four or five times a minute. And in the case of one thirty-nine-year-old woman, her obsessional and fearful thoughts about insects took a gradual hold after she had discovered woodworm in her bedroom furniture. 'Instead of them just being a pest that can be squashed or exterminated,' she said, 'to me they became an evil enemy, about to destroy everything. They were on my mind all the time at work and home. I kept searching my house – even when we got rid of the furniture and got new things. My boyfriend lives in a flat and, as it is occupied by men, the overall cleanliness leaves a lot to be desired. A few weeks ago I got it into my head it was full of bugs and fleas, and told him I didn't want to see him again. I get completely insane thoughts that even if I don't go to his home, he will come out with an insect on his clothes, transfer it to me, and I will take it in my house and they will over-run me. I didn't eat for two days, just thinking about it.'

In a case report by Leslie Solyom, in 1972, a technique known as 'paradoxical intention' was used to combat obsessional thoughts. Basically, instead of getting a patient to push obsessive thoughts out of his mind, he is asked deliberately to dwell on the thought, and convince himself of its truth. For instance, a patient with a fear of going insane was told to tell himself: it is true, I am going insane, slowly, but surely. I am developing many crazy thoughts and habits. I will be admitted to a mental hospital, put into a strait-jacket and will remain there neglected by everybody until I die. I won't even remember my name. I will forget that I was married, had children, and will become a zombie. I will neglect my appearance and eat like an animal.

All patients were told to use this technique whenever they had obsessive thoughts. It was explained to them that the more they tried to avoid thinking obsessively, the more they normally failed. So to reverse this process, they must deliberately think obsessively. In all, ten patients took part, with a 50 per cent success rate.

What must not be forgotten is that depression is usually a strong underlying factor with most obsessives. Success in getting obsessives to stop their thoughts, or their compulsive acts, therefore leaves them with a large empty time gap in their lives. At that point, they need a great deal of reassurance and help from both therapist and family to help them turn to other activities – or else depression will set in once again.

Obsessives are prey to far more indecision and doubt than the average person. Many people, for instance, when leaving for the office or going on holiday, will have a moment of indecisiveness that leads them to return and check the gas is really off, but an obsessive will check, re-check and then check again. As Leon Salzman says, in *The Obsessive Personality*, doubting 'often comes to play a most prominent role and overshadows all other elements in the obsessional's living. At times it may be so severe that the person doubts that he has really taken a breath or performed a task which, in fact, he may have completed only a moment ago.'

As an example of this, one obsessive told me that she always had to wash her hands before putting anything into the spin dryer: 'If I can't remember whether I have done so or not, I think to myself, "Well, it doesn't matter, I'll put it out to dry, anyway." Then I start worrying and despite saying it doesn't matter, it goes round and round in the back of my mind. I have no peace until I wash it all over again. This morning, I rewashed an overall three times.' Knowing I was coming, she had put covers on the floor of the hall and on the chair I was sitting on, to prevent my contaminating them when I arrived in the house.

The fear of contamination, she told me, came on her gradually. So gradually, indeed, that she only became aware of it when her husband started questioning her about why she was washing her hands again, when she had only just done so. 'I suddenly thought, "My goodness, so I am." And then I found I couldn't stop myself. I couldn't at that time even open a drawer: I would have to wash it first before I could take anything out. I think it hit me suddenly: "I have gone mad." It comes as a shock when you suddenly realise. I shut up like a clam and withdrew into myself: I didn't want to know.

'At first you keep quiet, and do not tell anyone. But, later on, I had to start telling friends because of our lack of social life. I couldn't have anyone here because of having to wash around the door and anything else they had sat on or touched. With the bathroom and loo, I had to wash around the walls and seat. It applied to myself and my husband, too. All the chairs had to be covered; and I would wash all the way around the door surround and handles. I am particularly fussy going to the loo and I always have to have a bath before going to bed. I also have to wash my hair every night. I can't have anything, like a cup and saucer, touching the bed. Last thing at night I have to wash the door handle, and my husband and I have to go straight from the bathroom to the bed without touching a thing. If either of us does touch anything, and then touches the bed, I have to wash all the bedclothes then and there.

'It's a living hell. Everything I wear is clean every day from top to bottom. It varies according to my panic situation. It's taken me the whole day to do any washing, because it may have touched a part of the spin dryer and I have then had to rewash it. This could happen half a dozen times and I could take a whole day to finish. The basket for the washing has to be washed and cleaned itself first, and the pegs and the line.'

At the very beginning, she had thought it had something to do with her marriage and had gone to a marriage guidance counsellor. Eventually someone had suggested she see a G.P. He, in turn, suggested that before washing cupboard drawers prior to opening them, she tried pausing and saying a prayer first (she was slightly religious). The suggestion did not work, however, as she was unable to stop herself washing every drawer before trying it out. The doctor then recommended a psychiatrist who, in a preliminary interview, told her that she was intelligent, that there was nothing wrong with her brain, and that he would put her on drugs. She took the pills home, but could not make herself take any of them.

Things at that point were very bad. 'I was washing and rewashing and I nearly lost control of myself. I thought I can't go on like this. I rang the doctor again, but he had just gone on holiday; and a friend suggested hypnosis. I was terrified, but what was the alternative?'

The sessions she has had with the psychotherapist, in a hypnotic state of deep relaxation, have, however, been of help to her – in that she is now able to practise this relaxation at home, and she finds that tranquillity lessens her compulsions. She herself prefers the more analytic type of treatment, feeling that if she had the behaviour therapy kind, where she had to touch objects she didn't wish to, she would get round it somehow, even if she was apparently co-operating. 'Analysis gives you a better understanding of yourself and your actions and reactions. The psychotherapist will sometimes use word association, both consciously and under hypnosis, and pursues any line that is triggered off. I know if I'm resisting, as I get a wicked headache. I realise he has hit something I don't want him to know about, and we go back and find out quite a bit that way.'

Last year, she and her husband did manage to go away on holiday for a few days. It was difficult for her: she had to wear the same clothes again, without washing them, and she hated getting into the bed. She carefully made the bed so that no one would touch it, and then came back to the hotel bedroom rather soon after breakfast one morning and found the room was being cleaned and the person cleaning it – after using a dustpan and brush – was leaning against the bed. She felt sick, but had to get into the bed that night. As soon as she came home, she had a bath, hairwash and complete change of clothing. But having got herself away once, she knows she can cope again. 'I am not prepared to live with these compulsions.'

The reason she had gone for treatment was that things had reached such a pitch that she simply couldn't manage any more. She was spending hours each day washing bedclothes, her own clothes, and cleaning the house. I asked her psychotherapist, John Edwards, in Reading, how a woman who declared she would not live with her compulsions had allowed them to control her life in the first place.

'Obsessives have very strong minds,' he said. 'People seem to think that this is a weak-minded condition, but it isn't. It's therefore very difficult to get the obsessive mind to go in another direction. All the obsessives I have treated are highly intelligent, but rigid and wilful; and all have a history of insecurity during their childhood. Indeed, the family background has been the cause in most of my cases.

'Obsessives have an overwhelming desire to do something which has been repressed completely by parental injunction not to do it.

This injunction has been so strong that they fear something terrible is going to happen, like the death of their nearest and dearest if they do it; and the way they think they can prevent it is by these rituals. They are a magical formula to stop punishment. Indeed, one obsessive has developed this idea to such a high degree, she thinks that unless she carries out her rituals, God, the ultimate power, will vent his wrath on her. Fifty per cent of the obsessives I see are washers: hands; bedclothes; toilets. It usually goes back, I find, to toilet training and guilt associated with repressed sexual desires.'

In one compulsive hand-washing case of his, the patient had started her rituals when she was only twelve. She had to wash and dry her hands three times; then repeat the whole sequence until she felt that whatever 'it' was had gone. When this ritual was noticed by members of her family, and stopped, she then transferred it to touching things, like various items of furniture. When that, in turn, became noticeable, she transferred it to looking at certain things for a certain number of times and got away with this for quite a long time. Gradually, she stopped of her own accord. But when she got married, she found it impossible to have sex, and started ritually washing her hands again.

What is really surprising is that so few of the marital partners rebel. One wife accepted that her husband's ritual cleaning in the lavatory took 32 minutes precisely each visit: 5 minutes washing himself; 7 minutes ensuring that the lavatory and seat were scrupulously clean; 20 minutes washing the entire place, including washbasin and taps. Another woman spent over half the night checking her clothes in the wardrobe, helped by her husband. A partner quite often co-operates with the spouse's ritual, in order to cut down the time it takes. Indeed, one obsessive's husband refused promotion, because of being involved many hours a day in his wife's rituals.

'A lot of the partners are extremely tolerant,' said John Edwards. 'I don't know how they live with it. The husband of one of my patients does go off the deep end, but his wife's reaction is so traumatic that it sets back the therapy. I get quite a lot of information about the obsession from the partner, as obsessives put up a lot of resistance to prevent you getting at the basis of their problem. They feel that, if you do, the catastrophic thing they are afraid of will happen. Usually, obsessives are very difficult to hypnotise as they dislike the idea of losing control, but the biofeedback techniques I am using at the moment help them to go into a very deep state of relaxation, which tones down the force of the compulsions. Once the patient is deeply relaxed, I then use various techniques – from deep analysis to behaviour therapy techniques – as no one method is equally suitable for all patients.'

Behaviour therapy techniques are now being used with reasonable success with obsessives. The principle is the same as with phobics – if the behaviour has been 'learnt' it should be possible to 're-learn' it. It is important, in fact, to make the obsessive aware of his behaviour – most of them have rationalised this to themselves. The aim of the therapy is to expose the obsessive's anxiety and prevent the rituals. Good results have been obtained by 'modelling' (getting the patient to imitate what the therapist is doing such as dabbling her fingers in 'contaminated' dirt) and 'flooding' (putting the patient, either in imagination or real life, into the situation he fears most. For instance, one woman with a fear of contamination by animals, had a hamster placed on her personal belongings and her hair). Both techniques are coupled with preventing the patient from carrying out his rituals afterwards. (One psychologist told me that he thought his patient was accepting this prevention rather too calmly, and on probing this found out that she had promised herself mentally to do her rituals twice as many times when she got home.)

Isaac Marks, in his comprehensive summing up, *New Approaches to the treatment of obsessive compulsive disorders*, gives examples of behaviour therapy treatments. In one case, a compulsive hand-washer, who feared contamination from his family, was told to bring contaminated objects from his home to the hospital. His room there, and his belongings in the ward, were then contaminated by these objects. Nurses supervised him continuously; the water taps in his room were turned off, and cleansing things were restricted. His routine washing was also supervised to stop excessive cleaning. The therapist visited him daily and made him touch contaminated objects – which upset him considerably and made him want to carry out his rituals.

He was persuaded not to do so. This continued for nine days and, during this period, the patient visited his home. Gradually, supervision was withdrawn, but observation continued. The water taps were then turned on; his family visited him; and then he spent several nights at home. After each step, 24-hour supervision was reintroduced for two days. The handwashing rituals disappeared and the patient's preoccupation with contamination gradually went. He remained well at an 18-month follow-up.

Another technique mentioned by Marks was electric shock treatment – the patients either shocking themselves before washing their hands compulsively or were shocked by the therapist until they touched dirty objects, at which point the shocks would stop. Rewarding a patient for touching feared objects, or stopping rituals, was another successful technique: in one quoted case, a man who avoided knives because of obsessive fears of harming people, was asked to hold a sharp knife for increasing periods, and praised for this.

Marks makes the point that improvement in hospital does not necessarily mean that the patient is better at home, and so treatment needs to include home supervision and support from the patient's family. Relatives need to be taught not to get too involved in the patient's rituals, and how they should respond to the patient's demands on them. Improvement requires a lot of effort – from both patient and therapist. A case illustrating this was that of a thirty-eight-year-old housewife, who had a 20-year history of compulsive handwashing and other rituals, centring around her fear of T.B. infection. These rituals became worse when her son – now aged two – was born. She could not feed him through fear of contaminating him, and her husband had to spend hours each day boiling bottles and feeding utensils to feed the child. The child itself was not allowed to play outside his playpen, and the patient's mother, who lived near by, was not allowed to play with the child for fear of infecting him, and had never even held him. The patient never swept the house, because she thought the dust contained T.B. germs, so a thick layer of dust covered most of the house. She opened doors with her feet, to avoid contaminating her hands. If her husband returned from work at all dirty, he sometimes had to strip naked outside the home before he was allowed to enter and then had to put on clean clothes once inside. The patient also had intermittent severe depression.

For treatment, she went to hospital for three weeks and was given relaxation treatment. However, she did not improve. On being asked to eat a biscuit which had first been rubbed on the floor, she refused – but finally did so after watching her therapist do so. She was also asked to rub her hands in dirt and to hold stained slides of bacteria without then washing herself. She proved very co-operative and soon began to lose her rituals. However, it was feared that she might not maintain this improvement once she got home – 200 miles away – so her husband and son were brought up to the hospital. The son was brought into the ward and the patient had to feed him after first touching the food on the floor. The husband was asked to help and his wife soon dropped her rituals concerning her son. When she left hospital, a nurse went with her on the train home. Once the patient was on the train, she started further rituals, such as avoiding touching handles on the door and windows. The nurse prevented this avoidance and, once home, got the patient to sweep the house, so that it was 'contaminated'. The husband also had to be taught to stop the cleaning rituals that his wife had ingrained into him over the years.

Rituals reassure obsessives that no harm will befall them. As this reassurance is very necessary to them, it is deliberately withdrawn during treatment. In one case, for example, reported by R. Hodgson and colleagues in 1972, a man who had worked as a lorry driver for six years was now afraid to drive in case he caused an accident. He also feared causing an accident at his home, which led him to check obsessively that the gas was turned off, razor blades safely put away and so on. These rituals made his life impossible and affected his previously happy marriage. During the first two days of treatment, he was encouraged to carry out activities which he had avoided for at least two years. He was also told to bump into people in a crowded supermarket and put pins, matches and a stone on the floor of the hospital lounge. At each stage, the therapist carried out the activities first, and was then copied by the patient. After each 40-minute session, the patient was told to resist his urge to check and not ask for reassurance concerning the possible harm he may have caused. He felt sick for a short time after each of the first 2 days of treatment, but recovered quickly and was free of symptoms after the 3-week treatment period. At a 6-month follow-up, improvement was still maintained.

In another case, reported by the same colleagues, a patient feared contamination by dogs. She always avoided areas in and around London where she had been 'contaminated', but regarded the town of Basingstoke as the greatest source of contamination. Before treatment, even a mention of Basingstoke brought on washing rituals. She normally washed her hands at least 50 times a day — using seven giant packets of soap flakes and a lot of bars of soap every week. She moved house five times in the three years before treatment in order to escape contamination, and threw away large amounts of contaminated clothing – especially boots – even though she could hardly afford to replace these. She also cleaned the house every day, including carpets, floors and shelves.

Treatment included shopping expeditions in areas she avoided, which mostly brought on intense anxiety and tears. With her permission, a trip to Basingstoke was undertaken, which severely depressed her for 24 hours. She was told that performing her rituals would interfere with treatment, and managed to resist excessive washing. A few months after treatment, she had to travel through Basingstoke; and though she felt contaminated for about eight hours, she resisted the urge to wash. She now goes out to work every day.

At the Institute for Behavior Therapy, in New York, obsessives are treated with similar techniques, also on an outpatient basis. When talking to Dr Steven Fishman and Dr Barry Lubetkin, co-directors, I was told: 'We get the patient to try to delay the time period before thinking the obsessive thought and actually carrying it out. For example, we get him to build in a lot of things to do first, like taking a deep breath, or going over to the window. Occasionally we use aversion therapy to stop rituals: we pull a rubber band or snap a rubber shock to the fingers, each time the behaviour is carried out. This is so negative that the rituals are often extinguished. But although we may do that initially, our eventual goal is to *wean* patients away from rituals.'

Brian Wijesinghe, Principal Psychologist at Claybury Hospital, Essex, starts treatment, in some cases, in the patient's home: 'I sometimes spend as much as five hours on the first session. What I do is supervise the activity. I don't necessarily stop all of it, but I ask them to do it in what I call "the right way". Recently, I went to a house where the woman was a compulsive handwasher. For instance, if she was preparing a meal, she would have to wash her hands in stages from the fingers to the shoulder, every time she touched something – whether it was taking the chicken out of the fridge, cutting up potatoes, washing the carrots and so on. To start off the programme, I was at her house just after breakfast time and began by giving her strict instructions as to the way in which she had to wash her hands, to help break the obsessive pattern. Following that, I got her to handle certain objects in the house which were considered by her to be contaminated. The seeds of fear lay in these. By doing this, she herself felt contaminated; and she was very distressed and anxious for over two hours, after which the anxiety started to subside. Her husband was then instructed to carry on the supervision. He had to take a week off work for this purpose. Her obsessions are now under control, and though she will have to be seen for some time, this is the essential breakthrough. We are now in a position to deal with underlying problems.'

Another obsessive who came to him fears contamination from outside the house. Anything, therefore, that comes into the house has to be wrapped up and put away. Even *letters* which come through the door have to be washed. She admitted that it was making life hell for her – and her husband – but although she came to ask about treatment, she finally decided that she could not face it, and would rather stay as she is. The problem here is that relations who are involved, like the marriage partner, do not know what to do. Motivation is all-important; so is mutual co-operation.

An example of this is given in *Contract Therapy in Obsessive-*

Compulsive Neurosis with Marital Discord by R. S. Stern and I. M. Marks. In this case, a thirty-one-year-old housewife had had a history of ritual checking since she was nineteen. She constantly checked switches and gas taps, and could not use her washing machine for fear that she would rinse 'coloured' with 'white' clothing. She could not wash herself either, believing this would cause her children to be harmed. Gradually her life became increasingly restricted and she could do no housework, or even wash or dress herself, without her husband's help. She became 'frozen' in the house, being too afraid to perform any action at all in case it led to her children being ill or dying from an accident. If she did force herself to do anything, she had magically to 'undo' the activity by using a phrase like 'God forbid'.

After the birth of her second child, the wife lost interest in sex and this, together with her husband's intolerance of her rituals, led to a deterioration in the marriage. The patient was first treated by group psychotherapy and then by prevention of the rituals at home for six weeks under the supervision of a psychologist. There was some improvement after this, but it was not maintained. Finally, 'contract therapy' was tried.

This started by the patient and her husband being seen together twice a week. At the beginning, each partner listed the behaviour wanted from the spouse. The husband wanted his wife to allow more frequent sexual intercourse and carry out more household work; the patient wanted her husband to have more serious conversation with her and complete the household jobs she had requested. Reasonable goals were then set up, for mutual reward. The husband emphasised that his wife refused to let him touch her breasts on the grounds that these were hypersensitive; and the patient eventually agreed to let her husband do this for ten minutes each day. In return, he agreed to complete home maintenance and carpentry.

· When they came for their second session, things were markedly improved between them. She was still inhibited about sex, however, and her next contract was to read part of a sex manual daily, and her husband agreed to decorate the kitchen if she did. As treatment progressed, the wife finally agreed to wash and then dress herself without her husband's aid and had less fear of doing the housework – although she still had thoughts about her children being harmed.

What is particularly interesting here is the relationship between the marital discord and the obsession. Attempts to treat the rituals on their own failed, and also had no effect on the marriage. But direct treatment of the marital discord improved both the marriage and the rituals (though not the patient's obsessive thoughts).

Leon Salzman, in *The Obsessive Personality*, says: 'The demands for perfection and the critical and derogating behaviour that the obsessional brings to a marriage may be too much to withstand.' An example of this could be seen in a letter in *Cosmopolitan's* problem page, which read: 'For two years I've been married to an attractive and intelligent husband. He has always been a great one for tidiness and organisation but in the past few months this has become excessive. Everything must be in perfect order and he will spend hours measuring drawers and cupboards so that everything is the same distance apart. I think he's getting worse . . .'

By keeping his possessions in perfect order, the obsessive hopes to keep his inwardly disturbed feelings in the same perfect order – feelings which come from strongly repressed aggression. But, as the letter-writer says, the ritual checking increases and gradually takes over the obsessive's life.

I watched this happen to one man who had a fear that he would get an ulcer if he ate or drank anything which had been contaminated by metal or fumes. He stopped eating a meal on his train journey into London and, because of the fumes, would not eat in London either. He used to buy goat's milk daily from a nearby farm and drink it – along with raw eggs collected in a wooden bucket – in the middle of a field. At one time, he used to drive to the farm. Then he took to stopping a mile or so away, changing his shoes (because of the nails in them) for cloths which he wound round his feet, and stripping his 'contaminated' clothes off on arrival at the farm, so that he just ate in underpants and vest. When the colder weather came, he paid for a special hut to be erected, made of wood. The first day he used it, the farmer's son flew his light aircraft deliberately low over the hut, causing him to leave his food untouched in case the fumes had contaminated it.

Sooner or later, an obsessive usually has to go for help; his life at that point being impossibly constricted by his rituals. In the same way, phobics also find their lives becoming increasingly restricted. Both phobias and compulsive rituals are techniques of defence against anxiety, and treatment is therefore closely related. But in getting rid of these defences, the patient is left with a very vulnerable personality. An obsessive, for instance, is being 'given back' many hours a day which had previously been spent in handwashing, or checking. Understanding and support are needed – both from therapist and family – to prevent the condition regaining the upper hand.

12

Phobic Causes and Treatment

One can have a phobia – as the list at the end of the book shows – about almost anything from snakes to string. But basically phobias fall into three broad categories. Firstly, fear of a specific object, such as a cat or spider. Secondly, a fear of a specific situation, such as being in a place, restaurant, school, or outside the home. Thirdly, and more abstract, a fear of a specific illness, or death.

Phobias in the first category – of a specific *object* – are often related to a previous, frightening incident. For example, a child who is already nervous of dogs could be knocked down or bitten by one, causing the fear to develop into a phobia. Or a child of a parent with a snake phobia may have modelled herself on the parent and 'caught' it. Sometimes a child under stress at home or school may have an unpleasant experience with an insect or animal, and transfer its anxiety to the creature concerned. The insect or animal may then arouse the anxiety and fear. Fears of animals, birds, insects and so on are almost entirely confined to women – possibly because up-bringing still dictates that boys should not show fear of such objects.

Phobias in the second category – of a specific *situation* – can also relate to a frightening incident. For example, a fear of being in a lift could be due to having been trapped in one once, or having been locked in a room. But social phobics – with their fear of social situations – and agoraphobics, with their fear of going out into the street, have more complex reasons connected with anxiety behind the onset of their phobia. Indeed, agoraphobia is known as the 'calamity syndrome' because it is so often a reaction – sometimes delayed – to the shock of the death of a parent or an operation, or a change of life-style. Sometimes these events are the triggering point of the underlying stress, or depression.

The third category – fear of illness and death – often starts by a friend or relative contracting a particular illness, like cancer or heart trouble. Sometimes the phobic has nursed a dying parent and then become morbidly convinced he or she will now get the same illness. A specific fear of death – not necessarily tied up with illness – can be a continuation of a childhood fear.

Much still remains to be answered about the causes of phobias. Why, for instance, should one girl develop a phobia of spiders after one is put down her neck when a child, while another, after a similar incident, remains unaffected? And what about those people who can give no reason whatsoever to explain their phobia? Why should natural childhood fears, like fears of strangers or the dark, remain after puberty with some, and not with others? And why should a build-up of stress cause agoraphobia in some instances, a nervous breakdown in others? Most mystifying, perhaps, is the sudden onset of hydrophobia after a person is bitten by a rabid dog.

Although the causes of a phobia may differ, the effect on all phobics, faced with what they fear, is the same – varying only in degree. They get a panic attack, with its attendant sensations: breathlessness, pounding heart, dizziness or fainting, tenseness, sweating, a feeling of remoteness. Their reaction is, naturally enough, to avoid getting into the same situation again. This is comparatively easy if it is just a question of avoiding cats, or heights. But if the panic attacks are the nervous system's reaction to over-stress, they can occur anywhere: a lift, a street, a restaurant. The person concerned then tries to avoid repeating that particular situation, which can seriously curtail his activities. He may also interpret these frightening sensations as symptoms of an illness, and go to the doctor for treatment, under the impression he is going mad, or having a heart attack.

The belief as to how a phobia, or obsession, starts governs the treatment and explains why there are radically different approaches to the problem. Few phobics realise or are told this, so when they are referred to a psychiatrist or psychologist, they accept the treatment he gives to them. This will be according to his beliefs, but not necessarily what the phobic would choose if he or she were aware of a choice. Unfortunately, practitioners of one type of treatment are often blinkered to any other method.

Some consider, for example, that the depressive side of agoraphobia should be treated, so they prescribe certain strong antidepressant drugs. Many patients on these drugs report an immediate, marked improvement. But the phobic should be told that there may be side effects and certain dietary restrictions, such as cheese and alcohol. A longer-term disadvantage is that a patient could become increasingly dependent on the pills and, unless the underlying reason for the depression and resultant phobia is treated, may not be able to give these up – or have to return to them from time to time throughout life. (Such drugs, of course, are quite different from tranquillisers, which merely allay anxiety.)

The analytic approach assumes all phobias come from repressed conflict, particularly conflict centred on childhood and early family relationships. The phobia is considered to represent a symbol of the real fear (for example, a fear of heights really representing a fear of downfall in one's job). Analysts try to find the real source of the problem, so that the phobic can understand this and change his thinking and behaviour.

In contrast, the behaviour therapists believe that concentrating on the roots of the phobia is of no great use. The patient may, they agree, be brought to understand why he is phobic – but this does not mean that he will necessarily be cured of his phobia. They, therefore, aim at changing his behaviour, considering that a fear has been 'learnt' and so therefore can be 'unlearnt'. The basic approach is to relax the phobic and then introduce him to the object or situation he fears in gradual steps, either in imagination, or real life, or both. For example, a spider phobic might be shown an imitation spider some distance away at the first session; and by the last session be able to tolerate a real spider quite near. The various methods used are discussed with the patient first, so that he is aware of, and agrees with, the course of treatment. The main techniques used are:

Desensitisation. The patient is relaxed – usually by standard muscular relaxation methods – and then, over a series of sessions, is asked to imagine what he fears in an ever-increasing gradient. For example, a plane phobic might start by imagining being at the airport and end by visualising take-off or landing. Sessions are not necessarily confined to imagination: patients may be shown pictures, or hear tape-recordings, of the feared object; and finally be introduced to the object or situation itself.

Flooding (implosion). This, done only with the patient's co-operation and understanding, involves the patient's immediate confrontation with the phobic object, without escape, until he becomes used to it. This can be in imagination or in reality. A claustrophobic, for example, might be shut in a cupboard for an agreed time. The theory is that, though the patient's anxiety level will rise to its highest level, it cannot stay there and must drop.

Modelling. The therapist carries out a particular, feared action, during treatment and the patient is encouraged to imitate it: for instance, a therapist would hold or stroke a cat, and the cat phobic would then practise doing likewise.

Group therapy. Group treatment, where members carry out techniques together, led by the therapist, but also talk out their problems and fears. It is particularly used with agoraphobics.

When behaviour therapy first really gained ground in the late 1950s, therapists were criticised for being hard-hearted and treating the patient as a clinical experiment rather than a human. Even recently one wrote sadly, with apologies to Flanders and Swann:

> 'Nobody likes a behaviourist much.
> If you ask the reason why,
> They will say it's because of his scaly touch
> And his cold and glittering eye.'

In fact, behaviour therapists now vary considerably in their techniques and most by no means ignore the phobic's present and past circumstances, as these obviously have a bearing on whether the phobia improves. Some behaviourists, particularly in New York, use psychoanalytic techniques if they think these helpful. But a certain animosity still exists between psychoanalysts and behaviourists: the former complaining that they have to pick up the pieces after a person has been apparently cured by the behaviourist; while the behaviourists claim they can cure a phobic by short-term practical treatment, after he had spent years 'lying on a couch'.

A vast number of phobics are also treated privately by psychotherapists and hypnotherapists, whose techniques can include both analytic and behavioural methods. Phobics can also try homeopathy and naturopathy – where the whole body is treated – as well as acupuncture. Biofeedback machines – an electronic means of monitoring physiological changes – can also be used by a phobic as a way of tuning-in to his anxiety level, and, with the help of the machine, lowering it. (Relevant addresses, from where more detailed information can be obtained, are given in the appendix.)

Those suffering from some of the more complex phobias often have problems even after apparently successful treatment. For example, agoraphobics – particularly those who have been housebound for years – have got so used to isolation that they need to be re-taught how to cope with life outside, like long-term prisoners. Dr Robert Sharpe of the Centre for Behavioural Psychotherapy in London (a private clinic, which cures some 85 per cent of its phobic patients) puts a great deal of emphasis on teaching phobics how to meet, and deal with, taxing situations. He feels that after being housebound, the phobic will have lost his social skills, and forgotten how to talk to the people behind the counter. The Centre re-teaches these skills: how to apply for a job, say, or a driving test. Phobics may think they are better, but their newly learned behaviour can deteriorate. They need to know not just that they can travel on an underground train, but that they can control their anxiety if it gets stuck in a tunnel – so emphasis is laid on self-management and coping with anxiety.

The Centre is the only private one in London treating phobics with a behaviour therapy approach, although this type of treatment is available at many psychiatric units in hospitals. Many patients dislike attending psychiatric hospitals, however, feeling that there is a stigma attached to going there, and not wanting to identify with the other patients. And many others are put off by having to wait literally months for treatment to commence, due to the severe shortage of psychiatrists and psychologists.

As the National Health Service does not have sufficient facilities, and general practitioners lack the required knowledge and tend interminably to prescribe tranquillisers, agoraphobics in particular are turning to self-help groups. Some of these groups last; some do not because of the difficulty of organising transport for agoraphobics unable to get out on their own (a factor which means that many can never consider treatment). Members exchange tips (like wearing dark glasses, pushing a shopping-wheeler, learning to relax indoors); and sometimes there are relaxation exercises, or advice from a consultant or therapist, at the meeting. At other times, these meetings are merely a social get-together to relieve feelings of isolation. In New York, there are more groups of mixed phobics being run – although these are always led by a psychologist or psychiatrist.

The number of phobics is apparently growing because as phobias become more widely discussed, more people admit to suffering from them, and also because general living stress is on the increase. What is lacking, however, is some co-ordinating centre which the phobic can write to, or visit, in order to get positive advice and information on the causes of phobias and the different types of treatment and where to go for them. The Phobics Society's long-term hope is to open such a centre which would co-operate with local authority services and voluntary associations. It would have social and therapeutic activities to relieve tension, and also advise phobics on medical and psychological problems.

The two main organisations in the phobic field, the Phobics Society (for all phobics) and the Open Door Association (mainly for agoraphobics) are both run with unstinted energy by their organisers, and are immensely helpful to their members. There are also myriad self-help groups around Britain, as well as some smaller phobic organisations. More could be achieved if the organisations were not so fragmented. It is estimated that there are some four and a half million phobics in Britain who need both reassurance and help. Without these, the numbers will continue to grow.

APPENDICES

APPENDIX I: USEFUL ADDRESSES

Mrs Katharine Fisher
The Phobics Society
4 Cheltenham Road
Manchester M21 1QN
(For all phobics. Area organisers throughout Britain, and membership details, available from Mrs Fisher)

Mrs Mona Woodford
The Open Door Association
447 Pensby Road
Heswall, Merseyside
(Concentrates on agoraphobics. List of area secretaries throughout Britain and membership details available from Mrs Woodford)

Institute for Behavioural Psychotherapy
22 Queen Anne Street
London W.1
(Private treatment for phobics and obsessives available at this centre)

Mrs Vanna Gothard
The Phobic Trust
25A The Grove
Coulsdon,
CR3 2BH

London Centre for Psychotherapy Ltd
19 Fitzjohn's Avenue
London NW3 5JY

British Society of Hypnotherapists
51 Queen Anne Street
London W.1

British Society of Medical and Dental Hypnosis
10 Chillerton Road
London SW17

British Homoeopathic Association
27a Devonshire Street
London W1

The London Homoeopathic Hospital
Great Ormond Street
London WC1

The British Naturopathic and Osteopathic College and Clinic
6 Netherhall Gardens
London NW3

National Association for Mental Health
22 Harley Street
London W1N 2ED

MIND (Charity for the promotion of mental health)
22 Harley Street
London W1N 2ED

Acupuncture Association
34 Alderney Street
London SW1

Maudsley Hospital
Denmark Hill
London SE5

It is impossible to list all the addresses of relevant organisations, as this could be endless; and some of the smaller self-help groups could close. The addresses on page 179 cover the main areas; and local Citizens' Advice Bureaux and Samaritan branches are also very helpful in giving phobics addresses to contact.

Records/Cassettes
'Hope and Help for your Nerves'
by Dr Claire Weekes
(Cassette or record) available from
33 Queens Gate Gardens
London SW7 5RR

Relaxation technique recording
Aleph One Limited
PO Box 72
Cambridge
(also available: relaxometer and other biofeedback instruments)

NEW YORK

Private treatment
Institute for Behavior Therapy
354 East 76th Street
New York, NY10021

Behavior Therapy Center of New York
111 East 85th Street
New York, NY10028

Hospital treatment
White Plains Hospital Phobia Clinic
41 East Post Road
White Plains, New York

Behavior Therapists are listed with the Association for Advancement of Behavior Therapy, 420 Lexington Avenue, New York City 10016. In addition to the various clinics listed below some University Clinics have Behavior Therapists on their staffs.

Payne Whitney Clinic Behavioral Services, New York Hospital
525 East 68th Street
New York City 10021

Long Island Jewish Hospital at Hillside Phobia Clinic
New Hyde Park
New York 11040

Behavior Therapy Institute of White Plains
68 East Post Road
White Plains
New York 10602

Behavior Therapy Institute of Sausalito
Sausalito,
California 94965

Behavior Therapy Institute of Beverly Hills
Beverly Hills
California 90212

APPENDIX 2: FAMILIAR AND RARE PHOBIAS

Air	Aerophobia
Animals	Zoophobia
Auroral lights	Auroraphobia
Bacteria	Bacteriophobia, microbiophobia
Beards	Pogonophobia
Bees	Apiphobia, melissophobia
Being afraid	Phobophobia
Being alone	Autophobia, monophobia, eremophobia
Being beaten	Rhabdophobia
Being bound	Merinthophobia
Being buried alive	Taphophobia
Being dirty	Automysophobia
Being egotistical	Autophobia
Being scratched	Amychophobia
Being stared at	Scopophobia
Birds	Ornithophobia
Blood	Hematophobia
Blushing	Ereuthophobia
Books	Bibliophobia
Cancer	Cancerophobia, carcinomatophobia
Cats	Ailurophobia, gatophobia
Certain name	Onomatophobia
Chickens	Alektorophobia
Childbirth	Tocophobia
Children	Pediophobia
China	Sinophobia
Choking	Pnigophobia
Cholera	Cholerophobia
Churches	Ecclesiaphobia
Clouds	Nephophobia
Cold	Psychrophobia, frigophobia
Colours	Chromatophobia
Corpse	Necrophobia
Crossing a bridge	Gephyrophobia
Crowds	Ochlophobia
Crystals	Crystallophobia
Dampness	Hygrophobia
Darkness	Achluophobia, nyctophobia

Dawn	Eosophobia
Daylight	Phengophobia
Death	Necrophobia, thanatophobia
Deformity	Dysmorphophobia
Demons, devils	Demonophobia
Depth	Bathophobia
Dirt	Mysophobia, rhypophobia
Disease	Nosophobia, pathophobia
Disorder	Ataxiophobia
Dogs	Cynophobia
Dolls	Pediophobia
Draught	Anemophobia
Dreams	Oneirophobia
Drink	Potophobia
Drinking	Dipsophobia
Drugs	Pharmacophobia
Duration	Chronophobia
Dust	Amathophobia
Electricity	Electrophobia
Elevated places, heights	Acrophobia
Empty rooms	Kenophobia
Enclosed space	Claustrophobia
England and things English	Anglophobia
Everything	Panophobia, panphobia
Eyes	Ommatophobia
Faeces	Coprophobia
Failure	Kakorraphiaphobia
Fatigue	Ponophobia
Feathers	Pteronophobia
Fire	Pyrophobia
Fish	Ichthyophobia
Flashes	Selaphobia
Flogging	Mastigophobia
Flood	Antlophobia
Flowers	Anthophobia
Flute	Aulophobia .
Flying	Aerophobia
Fog	Homichlophobia
Food	Sitophobia, cibophobia
Foreigners	Zenophobia, xenophobia
France and things French	Gallophobia
Freedom	Eleutherophobia
Fur	Doraphobia

Gaiety	Cherophobia
Germany and things German	Germanophobia
Germs	Spermophobia
Ghosts	Phasmophobia
Glass	Crystallophobia, hyalophobia
God	Theophobia
Going to bed	Clinophobia
Grave	Taphophobia
Gravity	Barophobia
Hair	Chaetophobia
Heart disease	Cardiophobia
Heat	Thermophobia
Heaven	Ouranophobia
Heights	Acrophobia
Heredity	Patroiophobia
Home surroundings	Ecophobia, oikophobia
Home	Domatophobia
Horses	Hippophobia
Human beings	Anthropophobia
Ice, frost	Cryophobia
Ideas	Ideophobia
Illness	Nosemaphobia
Imperfection	Atelophobia
Infection	Mysophobia, molysmophobia
Infinity	Apeirophobia
Inoculation, injections	Trypanophobia
Insanity	Lyssophobia, maniaphobia
Insects	Entomophobia
Itching	Acarophobia, scabiophobia
Jealousy	Zelophobia
Justice	Dikephobia
Knees	Genuphobia
Lakes	Limnophobia
Leprosy	Leprophobia
Lice	Pediculophobia
Light	Photophobia, phengophobia
Lightning	Astrapophobia, keraunophobia
Machinery	Mechanophobia
Making false statements	Mythophobia
Many things	Polyphobia
Marriage	Gamophobia
Meat	Carnophobia
Men	Androphobia

Metals	Metallophobia
Meteors	Meteorophobia
Mice	Musophobia
Microbes	Bacilliphobia
Mind	Psychophobia
Mirrors	Eisoptrophobia
Missiles	Ballistophobia
Moisture	Hygrophobia
Money	Chrometophobia
Monstrosities	Teratophobia
Motion	Kinesophobia
Nakedness	Gymnophobia
Names	Nomatophobia
Needles and pins	Belonophobia
Neglect of duty	Paralipophobia
Negroes	Negrophobia
Narrowness	Anginaphobia
New	Neophobia
Night	Nyctophobia
Noise or loud talking	Phonophobia
Novelty	Cainophobia, neophobia
Odours	Osmophobia
Odours (body)	Osphresiophobia
Oneself	Autophobia
One thing	Monophobia
Open spaces	Agoraphobia, cenophobia, kenophobia
Pain	Algophobia, odynephobia
Parasites	Parasitophobia, phthiriophobia
Physical love	Erotophobia
Places	Topophobia
Pleasure	Hedonophobia
Points	Aichurophobia
Poison	Toxiphobia
Poverty	Peniaphobia
Pregnancy	Maieusiophobia
Precipices	Cremnophobia
Punishment	Poinephobia
Rabies	Lyssophobia
Railways	Siderodromophobia
Rain	Ombrophobia
Responsibility	Hypegiaphobia
Reptiles	Batrachophobia
Ridicule	Katagelophobia

Rivers	Potamophobia
Robbers	Harpaxophobia
Ruin	Atephobia
Russia or things Russian	Russophobia
Rust	Iophobia
Sacred things	Hierophobia
Satan	Satanophobia
School	Scholionophobia, didaskaleinophobia
Sea	Thalassophobia
Sea swell	Cymophobia
Sex	Genophobia
Sexual intercourse	Coitophobia, cypridophobia
Shadows	Sciophobia
Sharp objects	Belonophobia
Shock	Hormephobia
Sinning	Peccatophobia
Skin	Dermatophobia
Skin diseases	Dermatosiophobia
Sitting idle	Thaasophobia
Skin of animals	Doraphobia
Sleep	Hypnophobia
Slime	Blennophobia
Smell	Olfactophobia
Smothering	Pnigerophobia
Snakes	Ophidiophobia
Snow	Chionophobia
Society	Anthropophobia
Solitude	Eremophobia
Sound	Akousticophobia
Sourness	Acerophobia
Speaking	Halophobia
Speaking aloud	Phonophobia
Speech	Lalophobia
Speed	Tachophobia
Spiders	Arachnophobia
Spirits	Demonophobia
Standing upright	Stasiphobia
Stars	Siderophobia
Stealing	Cleptophobia
Stillness	Eremophobia
Stings	Cnidophobia
Stooping	Kyphophobia
Strangers	Xenophobia

String	Linonophobia
Sun	Heliophobia
Surgical operations	Ergasiophobia
Swallowing	Phagophobia
Syphilis	Syphilophobia
Taste	Geumatophobia
Teeth	Odontophobia
Thirteen at table	Triskaidekaphobia
Thunder	Keraunophobia, tonitrophobia
Touching or being touched	Haphephobia
Travel	Hodophobia
Trees	Dendrophobia
Trembling	Tremophobia
Tuberculosis	Phthisiophobia, tuberculophobia
Uncovering the body	Gymnophobia
Vehicles	Amaxophobia, ochophobia
Veneral disease	Cypridophobia, venereophobia
Void	Kenophobia
Vomiting	Emetophobia
Walking	Basiphobia, batophobia
Wasps	Spheksophobia
Water	Hydrophobia
Weakness	Asthenophobia
Wind	Anemophobia
Women	Gynophobia
Words	Logophobia
Work	Ergasiophobia, ponophobia
Worms	Helminthophobia
Wounds, injury	Traumatophobia
Writing	Graphophobia
Young girls	Parthenophobia

BIBLIOGRAPHY

INTRODUCTION

Alexandra Symonds, 'Phobias after marriage: women's declaration of dependence' in Jean Baker Miller (ed.), *Psychoanalysis and Women* (London: Penguin, 1973)

Sylvia Plath, 'Johnny Panic and the bible of dreams' (*The Atlantic Monthly*, September 1968)

AGORAPHOBIA

Eric Berne, *Games People Play* (London: Penguin, 1968; New York: Grove, 1964)

I. M. Marks and E. R. Herst, 'A Survey of 1,200 Agoraphobics in Britain' (*Social Psychiatry*, Vol. 5, No. 1, 1970)

David Julier, 'Phobias' (*The Practitioner*, January 1973)

I. M. Marks, J. Connolly, R. S. Hallam, 'The Psychiatric Nurse as Therapist' (*British Medical Journal*, 21 July 1973)

Claire Weekes, *Self Help for your Nerves* (London: Angus & Robertson, 1962; New York: Coward-McCann, 1963); *Peace from Nervous Suffering* (London: Angus & Robertson, 1972; New York: Hawthorn Books, 1972); 'A Practical Treatment of Agoraphobia' (*British Medical Journal*, Vol. 2, 1973)

SPIDERS AND INSECTS

W. S. Bristowe, *World of Spiders* (London: Collins, 1971)

Enid Porter, *The Folklore of East Anglia* (London: Batsford, 1974; Totowa, N.J.: Rowan & Littlefield, 1974)

Isaac Marks, *Fears and Phobias* (London: Heinemann, 1969; New York: Academic Press)

J. A. Hadfield, *Dreams and Nightmares* (London: Penguin, 1954; Santa Fe, N.M.: William Gannon)

Melitta Sperling, 'Spider phobias and spider fantasies' (*Journal of the American Psychoanalytic Association*, 1971)

K. Abraham, *Selected Papers* (London: Hogarth Press, 1927; New York: Basic Books, 1966)

Stanley Rachman, *The Meanings of Fear* (London: Penguin Education, 1974; New York: Penguin)

Brian M. Foss (ed.), *New Horizons in Psychology* (London: Penguin, 1966)

J. P. Watson, R. Gaind, I. M. Marks, 'Prolonged Exposure: a rapid treatment for phobias' (*British Medical Journal*, 2 January 1971)

David Julier, 'Phobias' (*The Practitioner*, January 1973)

Joyce Emerson, *Phobias* (British Medical Association and National Association of Mental Health booklet)

A. F. Fazio (*Journal of Abnormal Social Psychology*, Vol. 76, No. 211, 1970)

FEAR OF FLYING AND HEIGHTS

Leslie Solyom *et al.*, 'Treatment of Fear of Flying' (*American Journal of Psychiatry*, Vol. 130, April 1973)

Myron Denholtz and Edward T. Mann, 'An audiovisual programme for group desensitisation' (*Journal of Behaviour Therapy & Experimental Therapy*, Vol. 5, 1974)

Patrick J. O'Connor, 'Fear of Flying' (*District Nursing*, January 1972)

Arthur Janov, *The Primal Scream* (London: Sphere Books, 1973; New York: G. P. Putnam's Sons, 1970; Dell, 1971)

Karen Horney, *Neurosis and Human Growth* (New York: W. W. Norton, 1950)

SOCIAL PHOBIA

Social training: a manual (available from Maudsley Hospital, Denmark Hill, London SE5)

Brian Wijesinghe, 'A vomiting phobia overcome by one session of flooding with hypnosis' (*Journal of Behaviour Therapy & Experimental Therapy*, Vol. 5, 1974)

SCHOOL PHOBIA

David Julier, 'Phobias' (*The Practitioner*, January 1973)

Leslie Mildener and Bill House, *The Gates* (London: Centreprise, 1975: 136 Kingsland High Street, London E8)

L. A. Hersov, 'Persistent non-attendance at school' (*Journal of Child Psychology and Psychiatry*, Vol. 1, 1960), and 'Neurotic Disorders with special reference to school refusal' in Philip Barker (ed.), *The Residential Psychiatric Treatment of Children* (London: Granada, 1974)

A. H. Denney, *Truancy and School Phobias* (London: Priory Press, 1973)

Ronald E. Smith and Theodore M. Sharpe, 'Treatment of a school phobic with implosive therapy' (*Journal of Consulting and Clinical Psychology*, Vol. 35, 1970)

Charles J. Rabiner and Donald F. Klein, 'Imipramine treatment of school phobia' (*Comprehensive Psychiatry*, Vol. 10, No. 5, 1969)

J. H. Kahn and J. P. Nursten, 'The place of the child guidance clinic in the treatment of school phobia' in *Unwillingly to School* (London: Pergamon Press, 2nd edition, 1968)

M. B. Clyne, *Absent: school refusal as a manifestation of disturbed family relationships* (London: Tavistock Publications, 1966)

Philip Barker, *Basic Child Psychiatry* (London: Staples Press, 1971; New York: Jason Aronson, 1971)

THUNDERSTORM PHOBIA

J. P. Watson, R. Gaind, I. M. Marks, 'Prolonged Exposure: a rapid treatment for phobias' (*British Medical Journal*, Vol. 1, 1971)

ANIMAL PHOBIAS

R. Gaind, J. P. Watson, I. M. Marks, 'Some approaches to the treatment of phobic disorders' (*Proceedings of the Royal Society of Medicine*, November 1971)

I. M. Marks, *Fears and Phobias* (London: Heinemann, 1969; New York: Academic Press, 1969)

I. M. Marks and M. G. Gelder, 'Different onset ages in varieties of phobia' (*American Journal of Psychiatry*, Vol. 123, 1966)

Ben D. Monroe and C. J. Ahr, 'Auditory Desensitization of a dog phobia in a blind patient' (*Journal of Behaviour Therapy & Experimental Psychiatry*, Vol. 3, 1972)

J. Watson and R. Rayner, 'Conditioned emotional reactions' (*Journal of Experimental Psychology*, Vol. 3, 1920)

M. C. Jones, 'A laboratory study of fear' (*Pedagog. Sem.*, Vol. 31, 1924)

S. Freud, 'The analysis of a phobia in a five-year-old' (London: *Collected Papers*, Vol. 3, Hogarth Press, 1905; New York: Basic Books, 1959)

D. F. Clark, 'The treatment of monosymptomatic phobia by systematic desensitisation' (*Behav. Res. & Ther.*, Vol. 1, 1963)

J. P. Watson, R. Gaind, I. M. Marks, 'Prolonged Exposure: a rapid treatment for phobics' (*British Medical Journal*, 2 January 1971)

Ann Faraday, *The Dream Game* (London: Temple Smith, 1975; Harper & Row, 1974)

S. Valins and A. A. Ray, 'Effects of cognitive desensitisation on avoidance behaviour' (*J. Person & Doc. Psychol.*, Vol. 7, 1968)

B. Ritter, 'The group desensitisation of children's snake phobias using vicarious and contact desensitisation procedures' (*Behav. Res. & Therapy*, Vol. 6, 1968)

Donald Meichenbaum, 'Cognitive factors in behaviour modification: modifying what clients say to themselves' (Paper presented at 5th annual meeting of the Association for Advancement of Behaviour Therapy, 1971; reprinted in *Annual Review of Behaviour Therapy*, 1973 (New York: Brunner/Mazel; London, Butterworth)

CLAUSTROPHOBIA

Geoffrey Household, *Rogue Male* (London: Penguin, 1973)
S. Bryntwick and Leslie Solyom, 'A brief treatment of elevator phobia' (*Journal of Behaviour Therapy & Experimental Psychiatry*, Vol. 4, 1973)

ILLNESS, PAIN AND DEATH

J. A. Ryle, 'Nosophobia' (*J. Ment. Sci.*, Vol. 94, 1948)
F. J. Jarrett, 'Aversion relief using voluntary respiratory arrest: a treatment for phobias' (available from Dept of Psychiatry, Queen's University, Kingston, Ontario)
J. Wolpe, 'The systematic desensitisation treatment of neuroses' (*Journal of Nervous and Mental Diseases*, Vol. 132, 1961)
W. E. Rivers, *Instinct and the Unconscious* (London: Cambridge University Press, 1922)

OBSESSIONS

Leon Salzman, *The Obsessive Personality* (New York: Jason Aronson, 1973)
Leslie Solyom, *et al.* 'Paradoxical Intention in the Treatment of Obsessive Thoughts: a pilot study' (*Comprehensive Psychiatry*, Vol. 13, No. 3, 1972)
I. M. Marks, 'New Approaches to the Treatment of Obsessive Compulsive Disorders' (*The Journal of Nervous and Mental Disease*, Vol. 156, No. 6, 1973)
R. Hodgson, S. Rachman and I. M. Marks, 'The Treatment of Chronic Obsessive-Compulsive Neurosis: follow-up and further findings' (*Behav. Res. & Therapy*, Vol. 10, 1972)
S. Rachman, I. M. Marks and R. Hodgson, 'The Treatment of Obsessive-Compulsive Neurotics by Modelling and Flooding *in vivo*' (*Behav. Res. & Therapy*, Vol. 11, 1973)
R. S. Stern and I. M. Marks, 'Contract Therapy in Obsessive-Compulsive Neurosis with Marital Discord' (*The British Journal of Psychiatry*, Vol. 123, No. 577, 1973)
S. Rachman, R. Hodgson, I. M. Marks, 'Treatment of Chronic Obsessive-Compulsive Neurosis' (*Behav. Res. & Therapy*, Vol. 9, 1971)

A very influential new book is Dr Aaron T. Beck's *Cognitive Therapy and the Emotional Disorder* (New York: International Universities Press, 1976), according to Dr Zane of the White Plains Hospital Phobia Clinic – the oldest phobia clinic in the United States.